WITH HEART AND MIND

With
HEART and MIND

*A Personal Synthesis of Scholarship
and Devotion*

KENNETH L. PIKE

*University of Michigan
and
Wycliffe Bible Translators*

*William B. Eerdmans Publishing Company
Grand Rapids, Michigan*

First printing, November 1962
Second printing, March 1964

PHOTOLITHOPRINTED BY CUSHING - MALLOY, INC.
ANN ARBOR, MICHIGAN, UNITED STATES OF AMERICA
1 9 6 4

24115

PREFACE

FOR THE PAST GENERATION OR TWO THE EVANGELICAL WING OF THE church has viewed scholarship with suspicion. Reeling under attacks internally from higher criticism and externally from science, it has sometimes withdrawn into a defensive cyst formation in order to weather the storm.

But the price it has paid for defense has been severe. While accepting joyfully one part of the greatest commandment, it has often ignored another part of the same command. Vigorously, it has attempted to obey the command to serve God with heart and soul. Belligerently, it has sometimes ignored in the same command the order to love God with *mind*. Intellectual search aimed at understanding the dynamics of the physical world in which we live, at struggling to see the Christian responsibility to the increasingly complex social and cultural order, at locating points of contact and reinforcement, and contribution from or clash with current ideologies, philosophies, and scientific views — these struggles have often been abandoned. Those evangelicals who have dared contribute to or learn from them have done so at peril of disapproval from their own subculture.

Years ago, however, evangelicals were for a time in the forefront of scientific research. The impetus for modern scientific development, for example, came heavily through the Royal Society of London, the first of the great English-speaking learned societies. Many of its seventeenth-century founders were Puritans who, as their historian T. Sprat tells us, had "always before [their] eyes the *Beauty, Contrivance,* and *Order* of *God's Works*."

Can the devotion sponsored by Christianity be combined with modern scholarship as these predecessors combined the fervor and scholarship of their day? Some of us believe that it can — and must be, if we are to obey the Great Commandment in full.

My own struggle with the combination is due to the dual nature of my interests. I am a Bible translator. With the help of my colleague Donald Stark and others of the Wycliffe Bible Translators I translated the New Testament into the Mixtec Indian language of Mexico. In connection with the Summer Institute of Linguistics — sister organization to the Wycliffe Bible Translators — I have helped train others to translate. From these goals grew the necessity of rigorous scientific techniques for language analysis, both in theory and in practice.

The bulk of my writing and publication has been in various phases of language analysis — phonetics, alphabet formation, analysis of tone languages, and grammatical theory aimed at discovering universal principles underlying all the languages and cultures of the world. In these technical endeavors I have been — and am — fully a part of the academic world through an appointment to the faculty of the University of Michigan, as Professor of Linguistics.

The present essays try to let the reader see just a bit of the religious and philosophical struggle that lies behind the growth of this personal synthesis.

In Part One, I suggest that there are limits to and responsibilities from academic ability. On the one hand, the logical process gives to man a powerful tool; but it contains built-in restrictions in that it must start with axioms, presuppositions, faith, and language before the intellect can point out for us the consequences of these starting points. Truth seen through the logical process or in experience, on the other hand, demands action. If this action demanded by observed truth is rejected, then the intellect itself is corrupted by hypocritical feedback from such decisions. Acceptance of the power of God in one's life lays the groundwork for personal commitment to both science and Christianity, which so often have been in conflict.

In Part Two, I attempt to show how cultural views differ according to a viewpoint "outside" or "inside" a culture or society or philosophy or general system. Theological viewpoint is treated in reference to one particular problem which overlaps with linguistics — namely, the possibility of the existence of any true statements whatever. Moral viewpoint is seen in reference to God's laws as designed by Him to serve man rather than to tyrannize over him. Then problems of cause and effect, of guidance versus judgment, and of independence versus social and spiritual integration are shown to be illuminated by a Christian framework.

In Part Three, belief in God is shown to entail personal experience and desire for self-respecting character as well as intellectual components concerning the nature of truth. Yet commitment to faith in God and obedience to His will may bring with it disillusionment in terms of inadequate personal capacity, as earthen vessels, to serve as one feels one should — a distress which can be survived if one sees that God judges by the heart, not by outward success. This leads to hope in God's ultimate success in fashioning us into persons with adequate character, each of whom retains individual significance forever.

In Part Four, I point out the demand that in the Christian life the individual should have an outreach. First I try to show that one must not attempt to succeed by injuring others, but rather one must seek to serve one's colleagues and to help them to succeed in the struggles in life. This can only be done by putting others first — in a reversal of the human struggle to reach the top of the power hierarchy. As members of a team, under God, we may each find our place in the total role of Christian society.

As an illustration of the more personal implication of commitment to outreach, I then discuss some of the reasons why my own efforts have been directed toward Bible translation among small tribal groups in the backwash of civilization — in spite of difficulties of language, minuscule size of some tribal populations, and so on. Such a personal program — and any one of a variety of other possible ones — gives full rein both to intellectual and to devotional commitment which will eventually leave a deposit of service to God and man, and of growth toward the kind of character which I, for one, have as a prime hope.

Many colleagues join me in this hope — among whom is my sister, Eunice Pike, whose critical judgment has been brought to bear on many of these essays.

—Kenneth L. Pike

ACKNOWLEDGMENTS

THE AUTHOR WISHES TO THANK THE EDITORS AND PUBLISHERS OF the following journals for permission to reprint material which appeared in their publications:

The Alliance Witness: "When Failure Is Success" (95.5, Oct. 19, 1960)

Bibliotheca Sacra: "A Stereoscopic Window on the World" (114.141-56, Apr. 1957).

Christianity Today: "Strange Dimensions of Truth (5.25-28, May 8, 1961).

Eternity: "Prescription for Intellectuals" (8:11, 44, 45, Aug. 1957); "The Individual" (9.18-19, Sept. 1958); "Man or Robot" (to appear).

His, student magazine of Inter-Varsity Christian Fellowship: "We Will Tell Them, But in What Language?" (12.8-11, 14, Oct. 1951); "Why I Believe in God" (18.3-7, 32-33, Nov. 1957); "Serving Our Colleagues" (18.5-7, Feb. 1958); "Flaming Candle" (18.30, Apr. 1958); "The Death of Independence" (18.5-7, May 1958); "Intellectual Idolatry" (19.5-6, Jan. 1959); "All in All: A Linguistic Parable" (19.39-40, June, 1959); "Cause and Effect in the Christian Life" (20.33-34, Oct. 1959); "Players" (20.41-42, June 1960).

The King's Business: "Gold, Frankincense, and Myrrh" (48.16-17, Dec. 1957); "Walking" (50.10-11, Apr. 1959); "Why Angels are Curious" (50.12-13, Sept. 1959); "Why Is There a Moral Code?" (51.10-11, Oct. 1960).

CONTENTS

PART I: INTELLECT

Although one must use his mind vigorously for fullness of life, for personal satisfaction, and for service to God, there are limits to what can be achieved by logical techniques. Before the logic "machine" can work it must have fed into it axioms and raw materials for thought. If one forgets these limitations, then mental ability will be trusted to provide results that it is inherently incapable of giving, and it will become hostile to Christian truth.

1 The Logical Process and Christianity

THE ACADEMIC PROCESS — OR THE LOGICAL PROCESS AS SUCH — IS, I believe, in some sense, hostile to Christianity. If this be true (and it is debatable), the question is, why is it true? or to what degree is it true? Many of us wish to see a rational defense of Christianity; we are convinced that to accept Christian beliefs is an intelligent decision. We urge Christian students to enter more vigorously into scientific research and production. How can the academic goals at one and the same time be desirable yet hostile?

Since I Corinthians 1:21 states that "in the wisdom of God the world by wisdom knew not God," we assume that one cannot reach God exclusively through the logical process alone. In verse 18 we are told that to the wise the preaching of the cross is foolishness; in verse 23 we see that Christianity appears foolish to the Greek, to the wise, to the logician; in verse 19, that God will destroy the wisdom of the wise; in verses 26, 27 that "not many wise men after the flesh, not many mighty, not many noble, are called; but God hath chosen the foolish things of the world to confound the wise."

In Luke 10:21, to my astonishment (and I have been astonished about this for a long time, pondering on it, wondering what it could mean and why), we see that Jesus rejoiced that the Lord has hidden "these things from the wise and prudent," and has "revealed them unto babes." He was rejoicing that revelation has built-in filters which prevent its light from getting through to the man who is exclusively committed to assumptions of his own choosing. Windows, for this light to enter the soul, are built of humble readiness to learn from a Higher Source. Pride of self-contained intellect has no windows for outside light to enter.

What is there about the academic process which makes it hostile to Christianity? Why is it that "not many wise are called"?

How does logical commitment threaten to lead to closure of soul? The mind of man is not big enough to analyze all the world at once. The intellectual process, therefore, in order to study and handle something scientifically, first abstracts a small body of material out of the whole and studies that restricted bit. When, however, the components of a sample are separated for study, something may happen which destroys the whole.

Supposing, for example, one analyzes a frog logically. Its four feet are put in one pile, its two eyes in another, its other parts are logically distributed. The parts have been classified and in this sense analyzed — but if we now ask the frog to jump, he will not do so efficiently. This, it seems to me, gives a picture, however crude, of the logical process at its best — not at its worst — in the sense that logic always abstracts, always compartmentalizes, and is never fully able to put the frog together again.

As another step in the academic process, the scientist generalizes on his small sample so as to cover all similar data. He makes a graph of gravity, for example. He observes a falling apple; he studies its increasing speed; he studies the attraction of bodies; and then he says (if he's a Newton) that all bodies attract each other with equal force relative to mass and distance. Thus, the moon is attracted to the earth, and it keeps falling, but the rate and nature of the fall is such that it keeps falling "around" the earth. This also explains the earth's going around the sun. This explains movements of the galaxies. Suddenly the whole world is illuminated and enclosed in a generalization.

Science has such generalizations at its heart. If we start with such a generalization, and set it up as a curve on a graph, the brain then inevitably, I think, extends the curve, and applies it to extended areas. At this point the scientist may become dazzled, as he extends the graph to take in the whole world. He receives tremendous intellectual excitement, a feeling that he can understand the farthest reaches of the universe. This, in principle, may be what happens when a naturalist adopts as a philosophy a theory of, say, "naturalism," or "determinism," or "behaviorism." He has taken a small sample of material, applied the theory to that bit of data, and extended it, in general, to the rest of the world.

One more thing may then happen. He may forget (or willfully ignore) that at the beginning he abstracted something from the whole, and left some things out of his theorizing. For example, the determinist who writes a book to prove to us that we are wrong if we fail to accept the "truth" that "all behavior is determined," may forget that he himself decided to write that book, and that he believes what is in it to be "true." He is not easily persuaded that his insight into the material in his book is just the result of his diet, or of the impact on him of various conversations, etc. He forgets the "as if" of his initial incomplete sample and makes a complete belief-universe out of the results.

Once this is done, then there is no room for any other conflicting belief. Having abstracted from the whole a sample, having deliberately left to one side relevant data — in order to have something small enough to study — there is no place to bring that data back into the now apparently complete model. The scientist who studies materials and their laws may end up by having no logical place within his system for God. As the late Albert Einstein expressed his opinion — a view which led him to urge "teachers of religion" "to give up the doctrine of a personal God":

> The more a man is imbued with the ordered regularity of all events the firmer becomes his conviction that there is no room left by the side of this ordered regularity for causes of a different nature. For him neither the rule of human nor the rule of divine will exists as an independent cause of natural events.[1]

1. *Out of My Later Years,* New York, 1950, p. 28.

In accordance with working abstractions, the scientist may ultimately build generalizations, extend these to include the whole world, and have no room left in it for God. There is no room in it for God precisely because God was left out of the beginning sample. I think this may be one important reason why the world by its wisdom does not know God.

If we wish to swim in the ocean, we can jump into the middle of it from a ship, or walk out from a beach. We don't have to know where the boundaries are in order to swim. But if we wish to analyze the ocean, we dip a bucket, take out by careful weight one cubic centimeter, analyze it for gold, hydrogen, salt, platinum — everything that interests us. Then we draw a curve, a graph, and suggest that — if the ocean is uniform — we know what all the ocean is like. For the initial technical analysis, however, we have to start by drawing a boundary around our limited sample.

This is the difference between being a child and being a scholar. The child can be thrown into the ocean and — with some help — learn to swim without worrying about all of its boundaries. The scholar abstracts a small bounded whole out of the world and makes it his universe, and treats it as if it were the whole. If a scholar, therefore, is to get to God, he must start over again, with unbounded data. He must be born again. He must learn to swim, not excluding God from the physical world, nor attempting to control God with his mind by setting limits outside of which God cannot step. He must accept teachers who can show him how to swim, accepting by grace what God offers to him through Christ.

The problem can also be approached through a different figure of speech. Logic may be viewed, perhaps, as a machine which is designed, at best, to be such that when we feed into it certain data and turn the logic crank, we inevitably get certain conclusions out the other end. Logic is designed to give inevitably true results starting from known true — or assumed-to-be-true — premises. Logic is a wonderful tool when we want only logical conclusions. We should not reject such a machine merely because it is not equipped to handle all of reality.

The scientist who commits himself to use a logic machine is doing wisely, qua scientist, for use on data of science. But if he feeds into that machine convictions that there is no God, or ignores God because He is not in his corpus of data, and then draws from his logic the conclusion that God does not exist, his conclusion is irrelevant. Logic is a tool; it should not be made into a religion.

In my view, no one can be solely logical and get to God. I believe that there are paradoxes in life and faith which are not resolved by clean-cut logic taking care of — or providing — all the data. God's universe extends too far to be comprehended by the mind through the abstract mode of logic. I do not believe, for example, that I shall ever be completely happy about an attempted reconciliation of freedom of the will and the sovereignty of God in a single totally logical system.

Young scholars are expected to use the logic machine. As they see the conclusions implied by that machine, people will ask them, "Don't you think you ought to be honest?" This can be translated as, "Don't you think you ought, inevitably, to commit yourself to the logical results of your own machine — or of mine?"

My answer is, "Not always — but sometimes." There may be deficiencies in the logic machine. Or it may be that the machine is efficient, but only within narrow limits. Be honest — how? By committing ourselves to a mechanistic model? No, not if it is taken to represent the whole universe. Yes, if the "as if" of provisional procedure is never forgotten. Science needs such models. But behind them must be convictions as to the non-mechanistic nature of man — e.g., that he is the one who is employing the logic machine.

The universe extends beyond the mind of man, and is more complex than the small sample he can study. God cannot be reduced to a sample for analysis. At some point, we must admit: "We cannot know God by the academic process alone."

Christianity points up responsibility and demands action. Truth, including pre-Christian truth no matter how dimly grasped, tries to elicit action as a result. The person who through pride refuses to follow this imperative will find the light diminish no matter how dim it was to begin with. The price that a man pays for refusing to act on the truth as he sees it is to be led to believe untruth to avoid guilt.

2 Truth and Responsibility

TRUTH OF ANY KIND, WHEN KNOWN, DEMANDS RESPONSIBLE ACTION. When a person refuses to accept this responsibility that comes with knowledge of truth, his failure has personal and social implications. His soul experiences the consequences.

Since he had heard truth, Pilate had at least two responsibilities. First, he knew that before him was an ethical man, a good man, betrayed by jealous clerics. He should have withstood the clerics. Secondly, he had been told that this man had truth. The Lord in effect had said, "If you want the truth, you may ask for instruction." Pilate should have said, "Please — for me."

But he did not want to accept the civic and moral responsibility that comes with the acknowledgment that Christ has truth, so he used an intellectual dodge. He said, "What is truth?" If he could plead ignorance of the truth, he could not be expected to accept the responsibility to act in accordance with the truth. This was a very clever bypass, and is, incidentally, the best bypass used today.

There is no truth without responsibility following in its wake. If we reject that responsibility, we will ultimately embrace as true some basic assumption which is false. When a person refuses to *act* in accordance with the truth that is evident to him, he is rejecting the truth. For example, a scholar may reject truth in principle if he resorts to a clever piece of verbal legerdemain, rather than act, on occasions when the demand of the truth is clear, though all of its intellectual implications are not evident.

The basic assumption which Pilate embraced as true was, "It's not my concern what happens to Him. I wash my hands of it." But it was indeed his concern; he was responsible! He adopted this false belief, in my view, because he had refused to respond to truth which was physically in front of him and was intellectually teasing him to react positively.

If a person believes something to be true, which as a matter of fact is false, his conscience ceases to trouble him and he can relax. He can be completely sincere, but wrong.

A bridge doesn't stand up to a train going over it because the engineer is sincere in thinking that the buttresses have withstood the flood. The bridge stands up because the girders and buttresses upon which it rests are strong. One who is sincere is in a precarious position if the bases for his thoughts are false. And if he has adopted what he believes after a refusal to act upon what he knew to be true, he is, morally, in a serious position.

Some people know that they have the responsibility to do what is right, kindly, and clean; but they reject this by saying, "What is ethical, and what is absolutely true and good? Morals are relative, and, therefore, I am not responsible for what I feel is right." That is the way they dodge the demand of the truth and protect themselves by arguing around this demand. At this point refusal to act in accordance with truth causes them to adopt philosophical assumptions which will hinder them from the fullest truth which is open to them.

Experiments show that animals have a period of time during which they can learn certain behavior patterns important to them. As time goes on, some of this potential for learning decays and may almost vanish. Similarly, we are aware of the ease with which a child learns a foreign language accentlessly — and how increasingly difficult this becomes for him as he grows older. Perhaps, similarly, the acceptance of the truth becomes increasingly difficult with each passing opportunity to accept it. An opportunity refused at an earlier age may be an opportunity lost — for keeps.

The chink in the armor of resistance of the intellectual is his wistfulness for character — reflected in his near incapacity to close his eyes to sheer goodness in others who are under test. Hence our responsibility to live so that we can say to him with Paul, "Be like me."

3 Follow Now — or Perhaps Never

SOMETIME AGO MY ATTENTION WAS CAUGHT BY AN ARTICLE BY Hess about an experiment with some ducks.[1] An earlier experimenter had noticed that some baby geese had started to follow him all over the farm — and maintained this habit as adults — after they had been hatched in an incubator. They acted as if he were their mother. Why should they do so? How does early social experience affect adult social behavior so drastically?

1. Eckhard H. Hess, " 'Imprinting' in Animals," *Scientific American*, 198:3:81-90 (March, 1958).

Looking for the answer to these questions, Hess experimented with some baby ducks hatched in an incubator. He prepared some wooden decoy ducks — some painted with male and some with female colors — some broadcasting artificial noises, and some feminine calls. He set one of those decoy ducks on a six-foot circular track, placed a baby duck on the track behind it, and had the decoy move at a certain speed. Sure enough, baby duck walked along happily behind the wooden decoy. But when, after a while, he changed to another type of decoy, it would not follow that one. The baby duck would follow only the decoy of the type that it had started to follow early after hatching, even though the second decoy made more natural sounds and had motherlike coloring.

Then the investigators asked themselves how long it would take for a duck to get that habit. (They called it "imprinting" — the early formation of a social habit in a duck.) They found that sixteen hours after hatching was the peak time to set up this habit. When thirty-two hours had passed after hatching, the imprinting would scarcely work at all.

Thus they demonstrated experimentally that if they put the baby duck on a circular track behind a moving, wooden, male duck, that was the type it would follow. In such a way the pattern for its adult social behavior was set. It was imprinted at sixteen hours of age.

Now does this imprinting in the early life of ducks have any parallel in man? Psychologists tell us that the early life of a child is crucial for his adult behavior, for his adult outlook. Speaking from a different point of view, the Bible tells us that by his behavior during his life on earth a person is in some respects "imprinted" for eternity.

Perhaps that is why "another chance" to believe might not be useful or relevant in the next life. It is easier to understand why not, once we know about ducks. We are animals, too, and are imprinted. For us the life here on earth is equivalent to the first hours of a duck's life. But what remains of a duck's life is a short time relative to the eternity of our life.

"*Now* is the day of salvation" (II Corinthians 6:2). Why? Because God is cruel? No. Because He is a tyrant? No. He is neither cruel nor a tyrant. It's just that God permits the outworking of the law of cause-and-effect. We are animals that get imprinted with character. What our character is in this life, we will to some extent remain in the life to come. That is why this life is so important.

Ducks are born with the capacity to follow the first moving thing they see. We are born with the capacity to follow God. We can become imprinted by following something other than God. We can follow a "wooden duck." And it is disastrous if we think that such a wooden duck is God. Sincerity gives no assistance here — a wooden duck cannot take care of us. But because we have been imprinted by what we followed early, we may always remain with it.

We have considered imprinting in terms of being imprinted here on earth for all of eternity. But we can also get a lesson from the imprinting of ducks in regard to time spent here on earth.

Those of us who are missionaries should remember it. When someone comes to believe in Christ, who is the first moving person he sees that calls himself a "Christian"? *Him* the convert may follow — and he may be you.

It's fashionable in some of our circles to say, "We do not ask people to follow us; we ask them to follow Christ." Or, it is said, "Do not look at me; look at Christ." That is not wholly Scriptural. Paul told the Corinthians: "I entreat you therefore to become like me" (I Corinthians 4:16, Weymouth). "Be imitators of me, as I myself am an imitator of Christ" (I Corinthians 11:1, Weymouth). "Let all that you learnt and received and heard and saw in me fashion your conduct" (Philippians 4:9, Weymouth). There was no other Christian model, and it was built into them to follow a model. It is the same today. The first Christian a new believer knows intimately is to some extent for him "Christianity," and the life of that believer is what he is likely to take as the pattern for his life.

We should watch the pattern which we set. People are going to be imprinted soon after they are born. They are going to follow us. We ought to be careful. What we are, others may become. What we do, others may assume they can do.

Thus we understand that we ourselves are to be models, but the Scriptures teaching this should be balanced with others. For example, "Therefore be imitators of God" (Ephesians 5:1, Weymouth); "For you, brethren, followed the example of the

churches of God in Christ Jesus" (I Thessalonians 2:14, Weymouth). "And you followed our example and the Lord's" (I
Thessalonians 1:6, Weymouth). Christ is the ultimate model and
we should seek to make our characters conform to His. Re-
membering the lesson of the ducks, we should seek *now* to be
like Christ. We should seek now to follow Him, so that throughout eternity our characters will be imprinted in the nature of
the image of God in Jesus Christ.

And what if the seeking proves difficult? Curiously enough,
the amount of time spent in following the model did not affect
the imprinting of the ducks — but the total effort expended
was proportional to the result. Barriers to be climbed and
extra laps to be run made the pattern become more firmly
fixed. So, with us, vigorous effort in service may be more
fruitful in character building than years of merely sitting at
ease in the pew on Sunday.

When the ducks had lived past the thirty-hour time limit
before following anything, they were afraid of moving objects,
did not follow the model, and failed to get imprinted. So the
experimenters gave the ducks a tranquilizer. The result was
that with fear gone the ducks followed a model, but no pattern
was formed, even after effort and time. Even the younger
ducks, given a tranquilizer, were no longer adequately trained.
Evidently it takes some degree of anxiety to be imprinted! Is
this why the Lord leaves us in trials?

Perhaps a further consideration is related to our topic. Logical argument cannot be expected to persuade the agnostic. The
chink in his armor lies in his capacity to see — and near-inca-
pacity to fail to see — goodness working out in human character
under stress. When he observes faith manifested in integrity
and joy through temptation and injury, or sees a man without
self-consciousness or pride accepting deep personal loss in order
to protect others from cultural or physical destruction, he
seldom can be completely blind to it. This goodness is a light
on a hill which cannot be hid. "By this shall all men know that
ye are my disciples, if ye have love one to another" (John
13:35), unto death (John 15:13).

The wistfulness for character growth in himself, stimulated
by contact with goodness, may lead the intellectual to listen to
logical approaches which can help roll away the stone of logical

objection. The first responsibility of the Christian, therefore, is to live so he can usefully say, "Become like me," as Paul did repeatedly, as we showed above; the second is to give in words the report of the source of his hope.

If we cannot in good conscience — because of character defect — say, "Follow me," then it is time to change.

*With truth rejected, and an oppor-
tunity lost for growth in service to
God, other behavior patterns set in.
The mind substitutes trust in itself
for axioms which should come by
faith from outside itself.*

4 Intellectual Idolatry

FOR A LONG TIME I'VE BEEN INTRIGUED BY ROMANS 1:22, 23,
where intellectualism and idolatry are juxtaposed in an unusual
way: "Professing themselves to be wise, they became fools, and
changed the glory of the uncorruptible God into an image made
like to corruptible man, and to birds, and four-footed beasts,
and creeping things."

Earlier in that chapter, the Apostle Paul makes it plain that
these people knew about God. God had shown them His power
and His deity in some way (perhaps through nature) so that
they knew Him by indirect revelation. And yet they failed
to honor Him or give thanks to Him.

Instead they became non-theistic intellectuals, a step which
led to futility in their thinking. Their minds lost their former
basic insight into knowledge (their minds were "darkened"
since in the Judaeo-Christian view the fear of the Lord is —
epistemologically — the beginning of wisdom).

Rejecting the basic assumption of a personal God, they became fools in turning to worship sticks and stones.

Is it accidental that wisdom should turn into idolatry? It
seems improbable that things so closely tied together in sequence
could be unrelated. But how can worshiping sticks and stones
be related to intellectualism?

We seldom think of idolatry in our present intellectual[1] cul-

1. I am not dealing here with the desire for wealth, nor with intellectual
throat-cutting for status purposes, but with philosophical assumptions. If
the former were under attention, the Christian would have no doubt — the
Scriptures plainly refer to "covetousness, which is idolatry" (Colossians
3:5) and to a "covetous man, who is an idolator" (Ephesians 5:5).

ture. But are we right in disregarding it? Can human nature possibly be so discontinuous that idolatry, which was prevalent for so many ages, is absent from our contemporary intellectual milieu? The apparent uniformity of human nature in other respects makes such discontinuity dubious.

Perhaps if we rephrase the question, the answer will be more apparent. What in non-theistic intellectualism replaces belief in God? The answer seems to be that belief in God may be replaced by belief in an epistemology (a system of how we know what we know, and of the validity of that knowledge); or by trust in a philosophical system of reality; or by moral trust in scientific assumptions, explicit or tacit.

Before we go further, we should explain that we are not arguing that the existence of God can be proved to the satisfaction of one who resists evidences in this direction. The opposite would seem to be true, for assumptions based on faith are apparently an ever-present component in any system of belief — whether those assumptions include the existence of a personal God, or whether they begin with non-rational directionally-emergent forces governed by statistical probabilities. Our argument does not claim that evidences are so clear that faith is not needed.

We do intend to imply, however, that the choice of a set of assumptions is a moral choice. Adherence to an epistemology is not something which merely "happens to" a person, but instead it reflects a component of his moral development. In some sense he is, in my judgment, morally responsible for adopting an epistemology even though it can be neither proved nor disproved to the satisfaction of those who oppose it.

One set of assumptions is based on life as seen through "rose-colored glasses" with a bias which replaces God's view of the world. This leads to competing views of what the whole world really is like. It may, among various possibilities, lead to a form of pantheism. The total entity includes power, people, sticks, butterflies — a universe which is looked upon as either vibrant and alive, or placid and quiet, a big sea into which everything flows and merges. We ourselves, according to this view, come from such a source — like the pseudopod of an amoeba extruding itself into time and space.

Such a philosophy can lead to an emotional charge, an esthetic pleasure in which a person suddenly senses that he's an intimate part of the total universe. It can give him belief and a thrill in belief — a thrill which is related to the religious thrill received through sensing religious truth. Now as these philosophical systems develop, they may lead to labels, names by which to call the concepts included in them. Unless man has such terms available, a system cannot be developed very fully. Terms are "handles" necessary for us if we are to grasp reality and understand details of it. The nature of language determines that in general such terms will be chosen as analogies or figures of speech. So, too, intellectuals must look for a label for pantheism which includes its all-embracing character and something of the mystical religious thrill which comes from it. They may turn to the word "God" as meeting these requirements.

Within our Christian view of the world this clarifies the idolatrous nature of pantheism. For the adherent to such a "religion" reacts to nature as the ultimate source of power with a kind of religious awe and submission — an attitude which we insist should be directed only to a personal God. And as Christians we believe that such "worship" belongs exclusively to God as revealed in Jesus Christ.

As a linguistic process, however, this labeling is quite normal. Development of thought requires such extension of terms. Christians are subject to accusations of distorting "true" language when, in Bible translation, for example, they may be forced to utilize some vague term for deity (an "unknown god"), or to use an even more specific label of a locally defined god as a term to translate expressions for the God described in the Bible. The focus of argument, therefore, must not be misdirected. The linguistic process is normal. It is only on the basis of our prior Christian bias that we can say, as I am saying here, that certain uses of the term "God" in pantheistic contexts are evidence for intellectual idolatry.

Man grasps and organizes his world in terms of non-linguistic symbols, however, as well as by linguistic ones. He thinks in terms of flags, of diamond rings, and dollar bills. Word symbols may be supplemented by thing symbols. It should not appear strange to us, then, once a person has in part verbalized a pantheistic world view (in which everything merges and melts into the whole), that he should go a step beyond language symbols and find such a view hard to handle and conceive of without powerful non-verbal symbols to help him grasp it. Since man is a symbolizing creature, he may look for a symbol to represent this whole, and he may choose a molten calf, or a stick, or a stone. It is natural for man, who is a symbolizing creature, thus to symbolize this universe which he now worships.

This is especially true of the non-intellectual. The intellectual may be happy with his word symbols. The non-intellectual may in addition crave things as symbols. Thus as the intellectual idea of pantheism spreads to non-intellectuals, the unspoken demand for things as symbols tends to increase. It is here, it seems to me, that intellectualism can in fact become a bridge to physical idolatry, over a period of time.

This idolatry started with intellectual refusal to acknowledge God. Intellectualism replaced worship of God with pleasure and pride of intellect. Intellect created a philosophical system.

In this system intellectuals put their trust, on it they based their actions, out of it they developed their world view, and from it they received their emotional charge. And that was, and is, idolatry.

PRIDE

Vain blockade, this —
The haughty snow —
To interrupt
The lava's flow.

Past eyes demure
And face downcast
Pride spews
A lurid blast.

For Nicodemus, as for today's intellectual, an encounter with Christ may be the point at which new axioms point to new life.

The intellectual who starts with data concerning his own need for inner renewal, and with recognition that there is power in God through Christ to meet that need, can ultimately build a new world view.

This view provides immediate power for living, but leaves unexplained the precise technique by which the power reaches us, and the nature of the integration of this power with the laboratory world.

5 Prescription for Intellectuals

HAVE YOU EVER ASKED WHY THE LORD TOLD NICODEMUS, THE intellectual, that he "must be born again," but never is reported to have said it to the harlot, the publican, and the down-and-outer? If you have never thought of it before, think of it now. We repudiate any assumption that these reports in the Bible are just accidental, or that the Apostle John "just happened" to choose a particular illustration. To retain our confidence in the Bible, we must assume that this was not accidental; we must believe that it was designed. Studying the design, we note that to the intellectual Jesus said, "You must be born again," and He did not say it — so far as is reported — to the publican. Why the difference? There must be a reason, and I think that we can find at least part of that reason.

The down-and-outer who wants to be cleansed, forgiven, and straightened out, does not need extensive understanding of how help comes. He only needs help and needs it quickly.

If you are in the water about to drown and you come up and see someone, you call "Help!" and lift up your arms, and he reaches down and pulls you out. At that moment you do not try to figure out how he happened to be there, or where he came from. You do not stop to reason with yourself about whether or not his boat will hold you. You do not stop to worry about whether or not his help will really last. All you say is "Help!" and you grab.

And that is all that the sinner who is socially down does — the one who is helpless and knows it. The open sinner does not have to worry about whether the system of Christianity is logically coherent and airtight in its defenses. He only needs to see Jesus and to know that somehow He can help.

The down-and-outer who is in real trouble does not argue and ask, "Jesus, how can You help me? I do not see how it is possible. I am a sinner and therefore it is philosophically impossible for You to help me." The down-and-outer does not consider whether or not this particular help will cause any upset in his prior philosophical thinking. He knows just one thing at this point. He knows that he has been stubborn, wrong, and wicked, and he knows (by means of the Scriptures and the grace of God in his heart) that Jesus loves him and wants to help him.

We do not have to know all about the philosophy of Christianity to get help. It says in Romans 10:13 that those who call on the name of the Lord will be saved. It does not specify that those shall be saved who know that the crucifixion has the shed blood which, when applied to the heart, cleanses and that the resurrection made the crucifixion effective in us. A person does not have to know even that much. The Word of God says, "Whosoever shall call upon the name of the Lord shall be saved," and I believe it with my whole heart. All the down-and-outer has to do is shout "Help!" to the God and Father of our Lord Jesus Christ, and he gets it.

The same is not true for the intellectual. The intellectual already has his mental outlook logically formed, a coherent system with all of the pieces fitting together in a neat mosaic such that the removal of one piece of the mosaic destroys the pattern. The intellectual must be able to understand, if he is going to live with himself, from whence help comes. He reasons like this: "Ah . . . there is help offered us. Now just let us think about this for a minute. Where does it come from?

Power does not come from nowhere. It has to have a satisfactory source. Is there a source that can really contribute this power which is alleged to reside in the man Jesus? I am not sure of that. I wonder how we can test it. We look for it in our test tubes, and we do not find it. We get subjective evidence for it in that people say that they have received help; but others get help from psychiatrists and that seems to be of the same order of magnitude. Such help is all very well for those people who are slightly non-academic and emotionally disturbed. It is all very well for them to get psychiatric and psychosomatic aid through faith in this Jesus, but I wonder how it reaches them. Probably they are people who are used to relying on others. If someone promises them strongly enough that they will get help, they grasp on this, and their guilt complexes disappear."

He continues to reason: "And why does help come? Well, it is alleged that it comes because God loves us, but those who have studied the matter a great deal say that we are to glorify Him. Such selfishness in demanding that the whole world be subservient and glorify Him is something that we would repudiate upon earth. We could not allow this self-glorification in an individual, and to have it in God is abhorrent to us. We must have a more selfless God than the one the Christians talk about.

"And what are the implications of this anyhow? Christians imply an exclusiveness which is not congenial to our thinking. We know that in science there are often two points of view, both of which are partly true. One scientist will condemn another for years, and then we find that both were looking at truth; there was truth in both, but not complete truth. They were correct in what they affirmed, wrong in what they denied. Undoubtedly the Christians are in the same situation. Both the Christians and the Buddhists, for example, have elements of truth; truth in relation to an absolute, truth in relation to some kind of power behind the universe. It is too bad that the Christians have combined it with an exclusiveness and do not see that in the climate of opinion in which we now live this exclusiveness is unsatisfactory."

For the intellectual to get help when he is in that frame of mind is almost impossible. He cannot just reach out and grab a helping hand, because he wants to see it explained in terms of his system of thought. He wants to know the source of that help, the manner of that help, because he has already committed himself (consciously if he is a first-rate intellectual; unconsciously if he is a second-rate intellectual) to a set of assumptions that are rigid, airtight, all inclusive. From his point of view the system is complete; it is a whole, and there is room only for that which is already there, or for that which can come out of his assumptions.

Now, Nicodemus was not a pagan intellectual; rather he was a theistic intellectual, a teacher, a professor, an academician of religion. In Nicodemus' theistic system there was no means whereby a man could be good and at the same time claim to be God. He had an airtight system which he had inherited from his forefathers culturally. It was a good system. It included theism, it included God, it included power, it included the love of God. But so far as he was concerned, it specifically excluded anything which was not monotheistic. To him, a man who implied that he was God was also implying polytheism, and to him that implied wickedness or fanaticism. And there was no, absolutely no, logical point from which he could begin to argue himself into accepting a change in his system whereby such a man could be God. The intellectual structuring of his philosophical religious system absolutely excluded Jesus as God.

Now then, what did Jesus tell this intellectual? He said something like this, "Nicodemus, I am sorry I cannot explain it to you. You have seen something that troubles you; you have seen something that does not fit your system. You have seen right. You have seen me to be good, and you have seen me implying that I am God, and that I am acting with the power of God. This does not fit your system, but I cannot explain it to you because your assumptions do not allow for a starting point. Nicodemus, to you it is not logical, nothing in your system permits it. I am sorry that I cannot explain. You will just have to be born again." (Compare John 3:1-5.)

Now what did this mean? As I see it, Jesus' implications could be paraphrased this way: "Nicodemus, I am sorry, but I cannot explain this because you have no frame of reference in which answers make any sense. You will have to do without it. You will have to start without being logical. That is to say, you will have to start without fitting things into your system. And, Nicodemus, whether you like it or not, you will have to start with a jump in the dark, you will have to leap in faith into a new system. You will have to be born again. You will have to reject your old system as such and you will have to dive into this new one. To do this you will have to seize on the empirical data as a baby seizes on the things to which it reacts in a strange world. You will have to begin by seeing that I am good and that I have power. Rejecting everything else wherever necessary, you will have to build a new religious system on this starting point — on me. If you do not do this, you will never understand — you cannot understand. And, Nicodemus, you cannot ask me to explain why I am good, where I came from, where I am going, or what the results are going to be. You will just have to take it, and start all over again, although it smashes your present philosophical system to bits."

Of course, I have exaggerated the problem of Judaism, for as Christians we think we have a system which allows for it. But why did our Lord make Nicodemus wait for an answer? Because in order to understand Christianity philosophically as a system, the world had to wait for the crucifixion and the resurrection. Until the resurrection had come about, there was absolutely no chance to have a total philosophical system which made sense and included Him. Why did not Jesus give lectures in these things in systematic theological detail? He was not ready. The resurrection was needed. This, I think, is why Jesus had the doctrines of the church as developed in the New Testament wait until His resurrection. Then He had Paul show how the system worked.

But in the meantime here was Nicodemus, an intellectual with no hope of building a new system because he did not have enough data; with the apparent collapse of his old system, but with no hope of understanding the new. To him Jesus said, "Nicodemus you must be born again." Then He added this figure of speech, "The wind bloweth where it listeth, and thou hearest the sound thereof, but canst not tell whence it cometh, and whither it goeth" (John 3:8).

Why this particular illustration? I explain it this way, "You do not know where the wind comes from, but you set your sail. You do not know where the wind comes from, but you put up your windmill. You do not know where the wind comes from, but it will turn the blades and give you power." So Jesus said to him, "Nicodemus, I am in no position to tell you about the resurrection and the new kingdom. But if you will take it by faith, beginning with trust in my goodness and my power, you can get the power from God."

The intellectual needs to be told that his system as a whole must be replaced — that he must be born again. Christianity is not an accretion; it is not something added. It is a *new* total outlook which is satisfied with nothing less than penetration to the farthest corners of the mind and the understanding.

Some of us have been born again, but we are just babes. May God guide us that we not be content to be immature, but that we continue all our lives to look to God, that His power, His might, His love, His gentleness, His goodness, His unselfishness, His self-control, may penetrate our wills, our minds, our emotions, our relations with one another.

A long, painful clash can be traced between those who have thought to describe the natural world truthfully and those who have thought to live truthfully before God. Mind and heart have again and again sued for divorce. Scientists have proved so extremely successful in explaining to the technician the life of the world that they are likely to forget that they have been less successful in living as they wish. Christianity has been so successful in explaining to its believers the matching of their inner failures with the predictions of the Scriptures about failures, and the contribution of belief in Christ to the growth of desired character, that it has been easily blinded to the fact that it is not directly designed as a tool to explain the workings of the outer world. The respective triumphs of the two have made it easy for each to forget the contributions of the other and the need of synthesis. Occasionally, in the midst of tensions, however, the happy union is preserved. We must re-establish it for our generation. To this end the evangelical must deliberately join in serving research science.

6 Christianity and Science

UNTIL WE HAVE READ HISTORY, MANY OF US ARE LIKELY TO THINK that evangelicals have always been uninterested in science, under attack by science, and treated as country cousins by the intellectuals. When we study the past, however, we find that this is not so. Just a few lifetimes ago evangelicals were setting the pace in English-speaking academic, scientific work.

In 1667 Thomas Sprat was called on to write the history[1] of the then seven-year-old Royal Society of London. Part of the purpose of the book was to defend the Society against complaints from the ultra-conservatives of the day, who wanted to prevent Christians from studying the world on the ground that such study was injurious to the Christian life. The people in the newly founded Royal Society of England replied, "How can it be imagin'd to be a sinful and carnal thing, to consider the Objects of our *Senses;* when *God,* the most *Spiritual Being,* did make them all? Since they first were conceiv'd in his unspotted Mind, why may they not innocently enter into ours?"[2] This was the first great learned society in the English-speaking world — the forerunner of the American Association for the Advancement of Science, the Linguistic Society of America, the American Anthropological Association, etc.

And who were the men who founded this society? Although men of all religions were freely admitted,[3] as Sprat points out, nevertheless, a large majority were Puritans — spiritual ancestors of many of us who are evangelicals. Robert K. Merton summarizes the evidence at length.[4] In the early group which was a forerunner of the Society, seven out of the ten were "definitely Puritan," another was Puritan trained — but personal feelings not certainly known — and only one was clearly non-Puritan; of the "original list of members of the Society . . . forty-two of the sixty-eight concerning whom information about their religious orientation is available were clearly Puritan. Considering that the Puritans constituted a relatively small minority in the English population, the fact that they constituted sixty-two per cent of the initial membership becomes even more

1. *The History of the Royal-Society of London,* Second Edition (London, [1667] 1702). For extensive argument of the relation of evangelical doctrine — and of church — to science, see pp. 347-78.
2. Sprat, *op. cit.,* p. 369.
3. *Ibid.,* p. 63.
4. In a chapter "Puritanism, Pietism and Science," in *Social Theory and Social Structure,* Revised Edition (Glencoe, 1957). Further biographical comments on a number of the early men are found in Henry Lyons, *The Royal Society, 1660-1940* (Cambridge, 1944).

striking."⁵ These were a substantial part of that distinguished company of scholars of the generation which gave the major impulse to English-speaking science as we know it. In Germany the pietists — continental counterparts of the Puritans — were leaders in emphasizing the new science (e.g., Copernican astronomy) and bringing it into the schools, even though some individual prominent Protestants had opposed it vigorously.⁶ But since then the evangelicals seem to have been threatened — almost smothered — by science. What an extraordinary thing after "the Puritan ethic" had "canalized the interests of seventeenth-century Englishmen" in a way that "enhanced cultivation of science," with a goal toward "the glorification of God in His works and the control of the corrupt world"!⁷

One part of the change was due to internal attacks from higher criticism which — to many people — seemed to show that the foundations of the Scriptures were invalid in historical detail. This helped lead to theological liberalism. In resisting liberalism, the evangelicals developed as a protective barrier a resistance to scholarship in general.

A second line of attack sprang externally from the growth of the study of geology, the classification of plants and animals, and the study of the deposition of sediments in the sea and of old sediments on land. This led people somewhat more than a hundred years ago to begin to recognize a need for larger-than-expected time spans to account for some of the data relevant to the physical history of the earth. This clashed with the period of six twenty-four hour days of creation which many had held to be sufficient to account for the physical evidence and to be implied by the Scriptures. As the estimated periods of geological time began to lengthen, the Christian community was bothered intensely and many of the Christians repeated the kind of mistake that was made by some of our predecessors in reference to Copernican astronomy. Thus, according to Angus Armitage:

> But even before the publication of his book, Copernicus had been severely criticized by Luther, who, in conversation, used to de-

5. Merton, *op. cit.,* pp. 584-85 (based on Stimson).
6. *Ibid.,* pp. 588-89.
7. *Ibid.,* p. 574.

nounce 'the new astronomer who wants to prove that the Earth goes round, and not the heavens, the Sun, and the Moon; . . . The fool will turn the whole science of Astronomy upside down. But as Holy Writ declares, it was the Sun and not the Earth which Joshua commanded to stand still.[8]

Note, as a result, the caution given by the well-known conservative theologian Charles Hodge:

On the other hand it is unwise in theologians to array themselves needlessly against the teachings of science. Romanists and Protestants vainly resisted the adoption of the Copernican theory of our solar system. They interpreted the Bible in a sense contradictory to that theory. So far as in them lay, they staked the authority of the Bible on the correctness of their interpretation. The theory proved to be true, and the received interpretation had to be given up. The Bible, however, has received no injury, although theologians have been taught an important lesson; that is, to let science take its course, assured that the Scriptures will accommodate themselves to all well-authenticated facts in time to come, as they have in time past.[9]

Similarly, as a high-school boy, I followed intensely the efforts of defenders of the faith to argue for the fixity of species. But many Christian scholars now state — as Bullock from the University of New Hampshire does:

Meanwhile, one is ill-advised to champion the cause of fixity of species under the banner of Christianity. . . .

It has been shown earlier that for the conservative Christian scholar the synonymy of the biological "species" with the biblical "kind" [that is, equating species with "after its kind"] is not only unwise but completely untenable.[10]

Now the point of this paper is not to argue these matters. I have no competence in this area. What I am saying is rather

---

8. *The World of Copernicus*, Mentor Edition [1947], 1951, p. 94.
9. *Sytematic Theology*, I, 57 (Grand Rapids, 1871). The classical description of religion-science controversies is found in Andrew D. White, *A History of the Warfare of Science with Theology* (New York, [1895] 1955). For the first part of the twentieth century, see Maynard Shipley, *The War on Modern Science* (New York, 1927). For careful attempt to access the implications of modern science for selected problems of theology, see E. L. Mascall, *Christian Theology and Natural Science* (London, 1957).
10. *Evolution and Christian Thought Today*, edited by Russell L. Mixter (Grand Rapids, 1959), pp. 113, 118.

this: the scientists have indeed won some triumphs, forcing the church against its will to change some of its Biblical interpretations; and science seems to permeate the atmosphere of our general intellectual climate. What is our cue now? What should we do?

As I see it, there are two possible answers. One is to deliberately set out to attack science as such; to try to defend the faith by overthrowing scholarship. This method cannot win. Another — and vastly better — way is perhaps suggested for us in Jeremiah 27:6, 8 and 29:5, 6:

> Now have I given all these lands into the hand of Nebuchadnezzar the king of Babylon, my servant.

> The nation and kingdom which will not serve the same Nebuchadnezzar the king of Babylon, and that will not put their neck under the yoke of the king of Babylon, that nation will I punish.

> Build ye houses, and dwell in them; and plant gardens, and eat the fruit of them.

That was the way God had of telling them that the captivity was going to last a while and that they must learn to live there. In those days Nebuchadnezzar was — in some sense — the servant of God and the Israelites were taken captive by him. Today — in a different sense — science is a servant of God and we evangelicals have been taken "captive" by it. The Lord commanded: "Seek the peace of the city whither I have caused you to be carried away captives, and pray unto the Lord for it; for in the peace thereof shall ye have peace" (Jeremiah 29:7). Have we prayed to God to *bless* the scientists working in biology? Have we asked God to give wisdom to the astronomers who are studying light? It is the will of God for us to bless all who have given us a bitter time, in personal life, in war, or in scholarship.

We are expected, in addition, to serve science, our captor. God has something to teach us through it. We are not expected to go out and fight it. God has not put it in our power to destroy science — it cannot be done — but He has put it in our power to serve.

In doing so, we can look to the Lord to sustain the integrity of His Word, when properly interpreted. We need not fear for the "ark of God."

But what is service to science? It lies in the making of positive contributions to the world's knowledge about the world. Evangelicals need to enter eagerly into the search for objective truth — truth about the observable universe.

Christian colleges might well be urged to pray — and *pay* — for research workers to be appointed to their faculties who would publish studies in the technical journals. If these investigations are blessed of the Lord, they can become crucial to a growing discipline, so that they are used with appreciation by the non-Christian scientist in that field. They can support his investigations, and provide foundation for further work. When this has been done, the evangelical has served science. And having served, he will find a door open for witness to belief in the existence and power of the Creator of the universe. Let us not forget that the Lord told His disciples: "Ye know that the princes of the Gentiles exercise dominion over them, and they that are great exercise authority upon them. But it shall not be so among you: but whosoever will be . . . chief among you, let him be your servant" (Matthew 20:25-27).

Those of us working in linguistics have watched this facet of witness grow in the past quarter of a century. When some of us were graduate students, other students — or instructors — said to us: "So you are one of these despised missionaries?" or "If I could get you to see the folly of Christianity, my whole summer would have been worth while."

Today, instead of being met with discouragement, evangelical students interested in linguistics are often strongly encouraged by the same people. This difference is the result of two and a half decades of extensive professional publication in linguistic journals throughout the world. In that time, many members of the Wycliffe Bible Translators, through its sister organization the Summer Institute of Linguistics, have published extensively. More than one hundred and fifty of their authors have turned out over four hundred such items in which one hundred and forty different languages are discussed.[11] In addition, important and well-accepted publications have been produced by evangelical staff members of other organizations — by the staff of the Amer-

11. Data from the *Twenty-Fifth Anniversary Bibliography* of the Summer Institute of Linguistics (Glendale [now Santa Ana], Calif., 1960).

ican Bible Society, and by the faculty of the Kennedy School of Missions, for example.

The result is the salt's recovery of its savor. A door for witness has been re-opened to an entire discipline.

What God has done for one discipline He can do for others. The witness of the evangelicals producing professional material to serve their disciplines could — in some way unknown to us — grow into a concerted, effective effort.

If we could succeed in re-establishing the old Puritan academic-devotional witness on a broad front, a changed intellectual climate for graduate schools as a whole would perhaps result. Secularism would cease being the only academic option visible to many of the students of our universities. The new attitude would in time filter down to undergraduate schools and into the high schools. Scholarships and devotion would be resynthesized on a national front.

PART II: VIEWPOINT

A view from inside a system and a view from outside that system leads to different ways of perceiving it. Sharply different descriptions of a culture or of a philosophy or of God's ways of dealing with man result from attempts to see them from such different viewpoints.

7 A Stereoscopic Window on the World

Two Views of Swaying Branches

DIFFERENT PEOPLE MAY SEE THE SAME EVENT IN DIFFERENT WAYS. Last spring, for example, a few yards from the shore of an ox-bow lake which was curling through the jungles of the Amazon headwaters of Peru, I was listening to Esther Matteson explain some of the problems raised by the translation of the New Testament into the language of the Piro Indians. Suddenly she glanced up, looked intently toward the trees lining the shore of the lake, and said, "There's something worth shooting out there." All that I could see were a few branches swaying. "The wind?" I asked. "No," she said firmly, "the branches are moving too far in a small place — it must be either a monkey or a big bird. Oh, for a boy with bow and arrow!"

Miss Matteson and I both saw the same event — the moving branches — yet we each saw different events. Where I saw the trail of wind, she saw clues to the presence of meat to fill out a skimpy diet and to add flavor to the soup.

Explanation of such a simple event leads to principles which are very far-reaching indeed. They are central to the discussion of phonetics versus phonemics, the point at which the big break-through occurred in modern structural linguistics. They are vital to problems of anthropology, of perception, and of the basic categories through which we view the universe and know what we know. Yet the systematic application of such principles is just now making itself felt in the study of important areas of human behavior.

In the event cited, notice especially two ways of describing it. First, a detached observer might describe only the actual movement and setting of the items physically seen by both of us: the shoreline of the lake had growing on it numerous tropical trees. Within a cluster of these trees, at a certain place, a few branches were moving at such-and-such a rate of speed, such-and-such distances. This descriptive type, it should be noted, provides a kind of truth equally valid for application to Peru or Dallas, Arab or Indian, or sawmills, butterflies, and croquet. It gives a physical analysis of a physical event without necessary reference to the reaction of that event on one particular observer foreign to the environment as distinct from its reaction on a different observer who is by experience and participation oriented to that environment.

The detached observer's view is one window on the world. The view of the local scene through the eyes of a native participant in that scene is a different window. Either view by itself is restricted in scope and leads to a kind of distortion — the first, since it ignores the concept of relevance, or purpose, or meaning, and the second because it distorts or molds vision or experience so that one interprets what one sees, or hears, or understands, only through the rose-colored glasses of one's own experiential structure.

It is my contention that both views must be brought to the fore if any event is to be well understood. The student can get a far deeper appreciation of the universe of his researches, not by a "happy medium" attempt to strike a balance of description which somehow lies between the two, but by consciously approaching a topic from these two directions. Each approach may give a result so like the other that to the uninitiated they appear to be the same. Two pictures taken at a distance of a few inches apart have no interesting differences when viewed one at a time, but when seen simultaneously through a stereoscope produce a three-dimensional experience. Similarly, behavior studied simultaneously through these two approaches is seen in a much more exciting depth of understanding.

Characteristics of the Two Views

Since the analyst working in various areas with these concepts needs to refer to them frequently, it is convenient to have names for them. I have coined the term *etic* to refer to the detached observer's view, and the term *emic* for that of the normal participant. The labels are coined by utilizing the last half of the terms *phonetics* and *phonemics* which are current in the linguistic field in the approximate sense implied here, but with the new terms generalized to cover other areas of behavior. In political theory an act viewed etically has been called an "operation," but when viewed emically, it has been called a "practice."[1]

Several characteristics of an etic view differentiate it from an emic one. It is useful to list some of them, including those implied in previous paragraphs.

The etic view is an alien view — the structuring of an outsider. The emic view is domestic, leading to units which correspond to those of an insider familiar with and participating in the system.

The etic view is cross-cultural in that its units are derived by comparing many systems and by abstracting from them units which are synthesized into a single scheme which is then analytically applied as a single system. The emic view is mono-cultural with its units derived from the internal functional relations of only one individual or culture at a time.

The etic view is, therefore, classificatory or typological, since its units lead to a classifying grid through which each system can in turn be seen as comprised of units related to that grid. The emic view, however, is structural, since its units are derived from internal relations, rather than a potentially irrelevant but prior grid of relations. Hence the etic view approaches a new situation with units — or at least components of units — prepared in advance, ready to be found in that situation, whereas the emic approach leads to units which are known only after that particular situation has been analyzed.

Etic criteria are absolute, or — if somewhat relative — are relative to an a priori absolute or quasi-absolute grid. Emic criteria are relative to the place the units have in the particular systems.

---

1. By H. D. Lasswell and A. Kaplan, *Power and Society*, pp. 10, 25.

The etic criteria are frequently, therefore, measurable as such, without reference to the system in which they are embedded, while emic criteria are contrastive, and observable only in reference to differential responses which they elicit in relation to other units of the system.

Etic systems are the creation of the analyst, conceptual tools ready to be applied to data so that one can begin to observe them as an alien and reach toward an appreciation of the emic structuring of that data. Emic systems are discovered by the analyst, as units reacted to or constituting the reaction of native participants in events. Participants discover these units by being "born into" a system — by suddenly finding themselves in a series of events which they at first do not comprehend. Here they gradually learn to act as normal participants, as through contrastive situations (or by receiving instruction) they gradually learn to make the kind of responses to these events which elicit appropriate reactions by other members of the community. For a more detailed development of the technical implications of this distinction, as well as of other problems discussed in these lectures, see my *Language in Relation to a Unified Theory of the Structure of Human Behavior.*

The Etic-Emic Concept Related to Language Teaching

The explanatory power of the etic-emic concept becomes clear when applied to some problems met in the practical teaching of foreign languages. In English, for example, we have two vowels which differ sharply in the words *bait* versus *bet, pate* versus *pet, sail* versus *sell*, etc. To us, as native speakers of English, the distinction is very clear; so clear, in fact, that it seems obvious, to be followed as a matter of course. It comes to us as a surprise, then, to find that most Spanish speakers from Latin America have extraordinary difficulty in learning to pronounce these sounds differently. Even though the meaning of the words depends upon the vowels, they have a distressing time trying to differentiate between the vowels of *bait* and *bet* (and of *bit, bet, bat*, as well).

This difficulty seems even more astonishing when we learn that in their language they have similar sounds. The first vowel of English *halo* is very similar to that of Spanish *pelo*, "hair" (except that the English vowel in most dialects ends in a slight glide, and in some dialects has a lower tongue position), so that, for our present purposes, we may say that *pelo* and *halo* rhyme. Similarly, the first vowel of many dialects of English *Perry* is very similar to that of Spanish *perro*, "dog."

If, then, Spanish and English have the "same" two vowels in these instances, why should the Spanish speakers have any difficulty pronouncing the English ones? The answer lies in the etic-emic realm. Etically, the Spanish and English vowels are the same, or approximately so. Emically, however, they are utterly different. Whereas in English the vowels sometimes come in like positions in words — between the same pairs of consonants in *bait* and *bet*, for example — in Spanish the vowels are restricted in such a manner that the two occur only in different contexts. The first vowel sound of Spanish *pelo* never comes before the -*rr*-; and the first vowel sound of *perro* comes only before -*rr*- or in a few other restricted spots. (Note that we are talking about sounds, not about letters, or spelling, in which the two vowels are alike.) In addition, the sounds of *bait* and *bet* may in English, where they are contrastive signals, differentiate meanings, but in Spanish, where because of their special distributions they are noncontrastive, they do not differentiate meanings. The contrastive status of these two etically different English vowels makes them "emically different" as well. The noncontrastive distribution of the two etically distinct Spanish vowels, on the contrary, leaves them "emically the same" vowel.

This problem can now be generalized: whenever one language contains two etically different vowels which are there emically the same, speakers of that language will have difficulty learning to pronounce these vowels in a second language if in that second language they are emically distinct. This theoretical principle underlies a very large percentage of all recent development in preparing textbooks for the practical teaching of foreign languages.

Perceptual Grids

In the utilization of distributional evidence in the last paragraphs a further principle is hidden. An emic unit does not exist in a vacuum, but occurs only as a point in — and relative to — the larger system which it in part comprises. An emic system is not an unorganized aggregate of units like billiard balls in a bucket, but an interrelated set of units, each of which depends for its functional existence upon the concomitant functional existence of other units in the system. Just as one defines *son* in reference to *father*, and *father* in reference to *son*, so a vowel *e* functions in a system in reference to other vowels distributed within the system in contrast to it.

Now our own emic pattern of behavior heavily influences or controls our perceptions. We hear many components of a foreign language in terms of the emic units — and distinctions between units — of our own language. The Spanish speaker is not limited to difficulty in pronouncing *bit* versus *bet*, or *mate* versus *met*, but is likewise hindered from hearing the difference. He tends to reinterpret the etic data in terms of his own experience, and structural units of that experience, which do not include that distinction.

This emic perceptual reinterpretation of etic data (or of data emic to a different system) can be illustrated by tossing pebbles into a grid of boxes. Let us suppose that the boxes have the following shape:

Let us suppose, further, that the dividers are so transparent as to be invisible. The shape of the grid would nevertheless be determinable by the pattern which the pebbles form as they fall into it (grid A):

A different shaped grid (we call it B) would be deduced from the following pebble pattern:

If, now, we drop pebbles through grid B, but between that grid and the ground there stands the grid A, the final pebble pattern on the ground will be heavily modified by grid A. The spanish speaker, in terms of this figure of speech, has a phonemic grid A, listening to English coming at him through English grid B. The Spanish person still hears in terms of his own grid A, and mimics B in a distorted fashion by pronouncing through grid A.

Similar problems are at the heart of difficulties not only of language, but of understanding customs, ideas, or philosophical systems.

Education, to a considerable extent, is the process of providing the student a broad etic, cross-cultural (or cross-problem) training, with experience in a variety of emic situations and in discovering the relevant emic structure of such situations, so as to give to the student a flexibility which makes him less rigidly subject to his own normal grid. Training may give experience within one immediately useful grid. From this point of view, education as distinct from training must give the wider experience so that on the basis of broad etic knowledge the student will be pliable and perceptually imaginative when he faces a problem or an emic structure which differs from or is outside of his own emic structure. It is here, then, that the justification lies for giving linguistic lectures to students whose primary interest is not language. It helps to provide to all a stereoscopic window on the world.

It should now be possible to see that language theory, generalized here to etic and emic views, has many points where it touches on philosophical problems. We can mention a few, without attempting to discuss them. How does the language grid — the linguistic emic system — affect or determine one's perceptions of the universe? What characteristics of reality determine some of the limits of human emic systems, both perceptual and linguistic? Are there any facts observable by a human, emically structured adult which are not affected by the structuring of the observer? That is, are there any neutral facts with which to begin discussion? What is the relation of objective to subjective data, if objective data have concealed within them a component of human emic structuring? How do such considerations relate to those problems of physical theory in which the observer — as in the theory of relativity — must be brought into consideration? If all matters are emically structured, what prevents our perceptions from being wildly diverse, and what controls the certain presence of a common core of experiences in all cultures so that translation is possible from any one language to any other?

Missions and Cultural Grids

Returning now to immediately practical matters, it is possible to see from a stereoscopic viewpoint why some persons find it difficult to be friendly with people of another culture. They see people, customs, events, and problems only through their own emic grid. Whatever the source of this inflexibility — whether from narrowness of experience, lack of interest in others, or even a brand of selfishness — it leads to misunderstanding, cultural clash, inefficiency, or even serious harm to a cultural system. Damage may be caused by one acting from high motives but lacking the elements of love as found in I Corinthians 13. This love would lead one to go slowly, patiently, and unselfishly in dealing with others. Rigidity is one enemy of Scriptural love, since it may reflect a self-centeredness on one's own personal emic view of the world.

Such attitudes may lead to a new legalism, a new "circumcision," based on Western emic concepts of cultural norms rather than on basic Christian principles. In the fifteenth chapter of Acts it was not just a few items of the Jewish law which were eliminated from the list of requirements for the new churches, but the whole cultural system. Only continued matters of morality and worship were there emphasized as being necessarily retained.

Even moral responsibility, the Scriptures teach, is in part (but not completely, as Acts 15 shows) relative to the particular moral code built into a particular culture. In Romans 2:14, for example, the interpretation of the word *nature* which leads to localized moral law and conscience and responsibility must not at all be attributed to a genetic inbuilt device, since the moral code differs sharply from tribe to tribe. The universal existence of some code, and certain outside limits within which all culture codes stay (e.g., in the presence of some restrictions on sex relations, on the presence of some social-governmental controls, etc.) seems to me to be genetic. The details, however, vary widely (e.g., as to just what relationships constitute incest). In these instances, then, it is the local emic pattern, the culture, which provides the framework of code within which moral responsibility operates.

The missionary must learn that such a moral system, present in every culture, cannot be smashed without breaking a control system blessed of God to preserve tribes from chaos. Christianity as a moral system should operate like a yeast, entering a culture quietly, transforming its institutions, changing their forms to contribute more effectively to the culture. Christianity was not designed to destroy the individuality of individuals or of cultures. Just as a person unified with and transformed by Christ still lives, so should a culture be infused with the fruits of the Spirit to change by the service of God harshness to kindness, and any dirtiness to cleanliness, but rugged cultural values should be heightened rather than ruined. Only a careful attempt to avoid looking and judging narrowly through his own emic framework, along with an attempt to look at the heart (the internal drive of the emic structure) instead of judging outward appearances will allow this. Such an attitude, in turn, can only come from the Spirit of God who works most easily through a person concerned for others, a person who has an alert mind trained by stereoscopic vision to be sympathetic to cultural differences.

It should not be necessary to state that capable people are needed for such a delicate task of understanding a culture and carefully guiding it in its acceptance of Christianity and its infusion with Christian principles. It needs men competent and devoted both in heart and mind, and also in spiritual devotion, intellectual discipline, and personal friendliness. The best are still none too good when an entire culture may be at stake. But, if priority must be assigned, friendly, understanding concern outranks cold academic competence.

Revelation and Grids

Once we have seen that God has chosen to respect and work through cultural structures, many problems concerning the historic process of revelation may be seen in a slightly different perspective. God chose to reveal Himself within a particular culture, through a particular culture, by means of events occurring in that particular culture. He made His message concrete by incarnating it in an emic structure, rather than by a series of lectures delivered by messengers aloof from and not a part of the revealing cultural medium.

The "target" language in this communication leading to the written tradition in the Bible was a pair of languages of specific men — Hebrew followed later by Greek. The problems of imparting a message across the emic barrier lying between heaven's communication system — whatever that may be — and man's verbal system involved the restructuring of the initial message into the target emic system. The message restructured into human speech had to be cast into the molding limits of noun, verb, lexicon, and sentence structures — in short, into a Hebrew-Greek structural grid — while retaining its conceptual integrity and the faithfulness of its intended impact.

The restrictions of vocabulary were not divorced from limitations imposed by the cultural structure. On the contrary, each culture develops over a period of time a lexicon adequate for the discussion of topics currently of interest to it. Lexicon restrictions, therefore, should be viewed not as inadequacies of a language structure, but as reflexes of the limited experiences and interests of the members of that cultural community. A gap in psychological vocabulary is due in the long run, for example, to the lack of a psychologist in the culture, not to any supposed primitiveness of the formal language emic system as such.

It is at this point, then, that that portion of the revelation process which had a verbal goal was forced to a delay to leave time for the guidance of a developing religious culture which through the labeling of the parts of its ceremonials would be developing the religious terminology of ceremonial types and devotional experiences, while at the same time the record of personal success, failure, penalty, and reward would be building the historical points of reference which would serve as a language matrix within which the significance of Christ in a culture could be communicated. The fullness of time for the revelation of Christ Himself in a form intelligible to the local culture awaited this developing Hebrew language, culture structure, and concrete history. But that the incarnation of Christ into such a restricted society might be made intelligible, in turn, to a wider community apart from that first culture, the message medium switched from Hebrew to Greek in order to tap the lexical resources which were the product of an entirely different set of experiences and interests. Whereas the Hebrew experience led to the language of power, signs, and demonstrations of God's working in culture, the Greek philosophical interests paved the way for the growth of the explanatory vocabulary of the Pauline theology.

The revelation crossing the gap showed itself not only in the language and in the culture, but crossed the gap of basic nature through the virgin birth, followed by Christ's physical death and physical resurrection. This last event capped the progression of events which demonstrated the concreteness of revelation. The choice of a particular language, culture, and finally the incarnation as a particular physical event cuts sharply across any attempt to treat the Christian essence as a mere abstract concept, as primarily an ethical code, or even as a system of theology abstracted from everyday living. Christianity stands or falls as a living program, a way of life, made concrete in the life of man by the life of God through the life of the concretely living Christ.

*Revelation and the nature of truth
must be viewed in reference to the
structure of language. Language is a
tool adequate to provide any degree
of precision relevant to a particular
situation. To ignore the fact that a
general statement may be true even
though not expanded to ultimate detail is to fall into the conviction that
language can never avoid error and
— eventually — to destroy knowledge
and science itself.*

8 Strange Dimensions of Truth

AS ANY SCHOLAR KNOWS, A SENTENCE MUST NEVER BE INTERPRETED
out of context. It is pointless, furthermore, to suggest that separate sentences are true *out of* a context of linguistic and non-
linguistic experience. Recently, however, some theologians
have claimed that no separate sentence can be wholly true *even
in* context.

I refer specifically to William Hordern's recently stated position.[1] Hordern takes two approaches to make his point. The
first starts from affirmations concerning the social function of
language. The second deals with the presence of areas of meaning — of ambiguity — represented by the words of a language.

Information, Understanding, and Truth

As for the first, Hordern adopts the point of view that a
"proposition is a tool; it has a task to perform, and to perform
its task it must be spoken and it must be received."[2] Language,
as a tool, must therefore — he implies — do its job of affecting
someone *exactly*. Inerrant propositions must "come into the
understanding of the hearer, meaning precisely what the speaker

1. *The Case of a New Reformation Theology* (Philadelphia, 1959).
2. *Ibid.*, p. 58.

46

meant by them."[3] This linkage from speaker to hearer must be so tight that "to express infallibly what the speaker wants to say, we must also say that it is impossible to hear it otherwise than the speaker intended it to be heard."[4] He would conclude that "an objective revelation is not inerrant unless it is inerrantly received," since the "subjective receiver of revelation is an indispensable link in the chain," and, following Kierkegaard, Hordern maintains that "there is *no truth unless there is truth to me*" (italics added).[5] Thus "if there is to be inerrant revelation of propositions, the hearer would have to be as inerrant as the speaker."[6]

If we ask for the reason lying behind the adoption of this view of language, we find in his book that it developed as a challenge to what he considers the "basic premise" of "fundamentalism or conservatism" — "that what God reveals is information."[7] He maintains with "modern theologians" that "what God reveals is not propositions nor information — what God reveals is God."[8] Hordern rejects the fundamentalist view that information has been revealed to us by God on the grounds that this view implies "with stunning logic" that both the Bible and the interpreting church must be considered infallible.[9] This he considers impossible. He then replaces this informational concept of revelation with that of revelation as being composed of the direct knowledge of God.

We have no objection to treating the contact of man with God in Christ as being part of — or one kind of — revelation. We object rather to the total elimination of information from the revelation available to us.

Furthermore, we do not deny that language has social relevance and purpose, or that language is designed to communicate with and affect other people. What we deny is that language has *only* the one function of linkage from one person to another. We claim that it also includes the functions of

3. *Ibid.,* p. 59.
4. *Ibid.*
5. *Ibid.*
6. *Ibid.*
7. *Ibid.,* p. 57.
8. *Ibid.,* pp. 61-62; see also pp. 55-57, 68.
9. *Ibid.,* p. 57.

man talking with himself; of formulating ideas for himself; of *storing* ideas in sayings, legends, or libraries; the presentation of information or truth in such a way that it is *available* for others who *then* or *later* are or will be *prepared to receive it.* It is the pair of concepts of availability on the one hand and preparedness for reception on the other hand which seem to me to have been overlooked (or perhaps rejected?) by Hordern.

These omissions may lead to ultimate skepticism if pushed to their logical conclusion. Let us assume, for example, that a teacher of very great scientific competence gives a lecture today to an audience of young graduate students. A tape recording is made of the lecture. Members of the class are asked to comment on or to repeat the day's lecture. Let us suppose that none of them understood the lecture. From the point of view of Hordern this would not be mere failure to understand truth — it would be evidence that the lecture was *not inerrant,* specifically, and by implication would also be evidence that the lecture is *not wholly true.*

Three years after, when these same students have had further training, they listen to the old tape again. They now understand it. The material, which formerly was not truth, by Hordern's treatment would now become truth because it would have done what propositions are meant to do.

In order to avoid this conclusion, I would claim, on the contrary, that the initial lecture was in fact *true,* and was in principle *available.* It needed, however, *prepared receivers* for its adequate reception.

Availability would imply that in order for material revealed to be at least *in principle* understandable to adequate receivers, it could not be phrased in a heavenly language which was permanently opaque to all human beings. It might, on the other hand, be interpreted as being available only to persons with the proper experience. One component of such experience is available to people, on a natural level, if they can read easily.

Preparedness may involve a delay while further data is being made available through succeeding events. Understanding — but not the presence versus the absence of truth — would then be retroactive.

Understanding is not in the same *dimension* with truth. Jesus had some things to tell to His disciples which they were not prepared to receive fully at the moment, and which they would understand only in retrospect, but which I consider to have been fully true even before the disciples were able to understand these teachings. He stated that the Son of Man was to be killed, and was to rise the third day. The disciples did not understand this (Mark 9:31-32; Luke 9:44-45, 18:31-34), even though we now do. The written Scriptures were also at times understood in retrospect — as concerning the triumphal entry (John 12:16), or prophecies of Christ's coming (Luke 24:45). Similarly, lack of belief does not invalidate the truth of an utterance — as when Christ warned Peter about denial before the cock crew (John 13:38), or when the Jews did not "understand" because they did not "hear" (John 8:43). Nor does teaching in parables, partly hidden (cf. John 16:25), make an item false.

Christ, furthermore, claimed that truth came through human language. Even though "they understood not," He insisted that "he that sent me is true" and "I speak . . . those things which I have heard of him" (John 8:26-28). And "they have kept thy word. . . . For I have given unto them the words which thou gavest me; and they have received them, and have known surely that I came out from thee. . . . I have given them thy word. . . . Sanctify them through thy truth; thy *word is truth*" (John 17:6, 8, 14, 17).

Language, Ambiguity, and Truth

Hordern's second objection to considering revelation as containing true information lies in the fact that sentences can be ambiguous.

Specifically, he suggests that the sentence "God is love" (I John 4:8) is such that "we cannot consider it infallible" since "to many a hearer it will convey the wrong impression, because the word 'love' today has many connotations that cannot be applied to God"[10]; to get the desired specific meaning of love from this context many other acts of God in the background history of the situation must be pointed out. Similarly, in reference to the sentence "Thou art the Christ" (Matthew 16:16-23), he states that "far from being an infallible statement, even to the man who spoke it, the statement had an ambiguous mean-

10. *Ibid.,* p. 64.

ing,"[11] since Peter was rebuked for his further statements that seemed to have grown out of the immediate situation. Thus, for Hordern, ambiguity in a statement implies error in the statement itself.

If this were to be granted, it would follow inevitably that no statement is ever true. *Every* word has several different meanings — or, in technical terms, it covers an area of meaning — even though the differences be small. Each context in which the word occurs forces a slightly different meaning to that word — even if it be by an infinitesimal amount — in a way that the non-professional observer would not suspect. With a bit of thought, however, he can see that the exact physical activity implied by the word "drive" differs sharply in the phrases "to drive a car," "to drive a horse," "to drive a nail," and "to drive a point home." The ability of various contexts to force such changes of meaning is vital to the function of language itself. Without it no learning could take place, no translation could ever be made, and communication would cease.

Since scientific statements, as well as statements of the man in the street, contain upon analysis a diversity of meaning, it would follow clearly that Hordern has in fact rejected the possibility of any wholly true science. The turn of the wheel is curiously complete. Having, along with the liberals, rejected fundamentalism because it "semed to require intellectual hari-kari"[12] in its relationships to science, etc.,[13] Hordern has adopted a position which, in my view, in turn breeds intellectual hari-kari through denying full truth value to *any* of the statements of science.

Dimension of Truth versus Error

We now ask: how can we avoid Hordern's conclusion that ambiguity implies error? We can do so if we view statements as containing *dimensions* — as we hinted in the first section of this article.

The first of these dimensions of statement has *truth* at one pole and *error* at the other. We have in mind the ordinary meaning of the words "true" and "false." Truth in a statement is

11. *Ibid.*, p. 69.
12. *Ibid.*, cf. p. 108.
13. *Ibid.*, cf. also pp. 53, 60, 86, 92, 113.

based upon information which can be relied upon. Error and falsehood are reports of observation, information, or judgment which cannot be relied upon. In this view a true statement about weather reflects the measurable facts of humidity, temperature, and so on. A person who operates on the basis of such a report will find himself acting adequately. As Edward J. Carnell says: "The true is the quality of that judgment or proposition which, when followed out into the total witness of facts in our experience, does not disappoint our expectation."[14]

The Dimension of Magnification

A second dimension of statements differs sharply from the first: *we do not wish to apply directly to this characteristic of statements either the term truth or the term error.* The contrast referred to is rather a difference which may be called *high magnification* versus *low magnification*, using the optical term metaphorically. If we look at a fly under a low-powered magnifying glass we may be able to see the whole fly with considerable detail involved. If we wish to see much more detail about the structure of the fly, we must use a higher-powered microscope. The price we pay for this fine detail, however, is very great — the fly as a whole cannot be seen all at once. The *pattern* of the fly as a whole has disappeared from view. As others have said, one cannot find a face with a microscope. Similarly, as regards language, if one writes for a beginner an extremely intricate textbook on the laws of physics, including elaborate details, illustrations, reservations, implications, and the like, the beginner cannot adequately get information from the book.

Neither the detailed treatment nor one showing the over-all pattern should be called true as such, and neither should be called false as such. Truth and error may both be found at *each pole* of this kind of contrast. A detailed statement may be true or it may be false. Degree of detail in a statement is not of itself either true or false.

Language is adequate to accomplish the aim of communicating information at any level of magnification. One must not,

14. *An Introduction to Christian Apologetics* (Grand Rapids, 1956), p. 45.

however, demand that *simultaneously* both exhaustive detail and general pattern must always be presented. It is only God who is able to grasp simultaneously ultimate pattern and infinite detail.

The Bible, in general, chooses to have a low amplification in order to have a high concentration of meaningful pattern present.

No scientific statement, on the other hand, can ever reach an ultimate degree of magnification. If one wishes to claim that a true statement must have the highest magnification, then no scientific statement can ever be true — there is always more detail possible. To equate truth with magnification is to abandon scientific discourse.

The Dimension of Relevance

Degrees of *relevance* lead to a third dimension of statement. Contextual resolution of ambiguity can be viewed in this light. Contexts cause changes in the meanings of words, as we indicated above, but they also force the hearer's *selection* of those specific meanings which are relevant to the intention of the writer. In the phrase "to drive a nail" one cannot rationally assume that the writer means "to control the direction of movement of a nail by moving it with reins." Context provided by a sentence, therefore, can — and often does — eliminate the irrelevant ambiguity inherent in an isolated word. Context provided by a paragraph — or a whole book — can also eliminate ambiguities inherent in isolated sentences. The sentence "God is love," interpreted in the context of the Bible, is narrowed in the possible range of its meanings. Language, by context, is *adequate* to portray truth by using words each of which by itself would be ambiguous.

The technique by which language carries out its business of selecting specific, relevant, components out of multiple-available components has reference to the way in which words in context influence one another. The process is extremely powerful. Without it, no language could ultimately function, even though the process is not yet too well understood.[15]

15. Cf. Robert E. Longacre, "Items in Context: Their Bearing on Translation Theory," in *Language*, 34:482-91, 1958.

Sharpness of focus on some one relevant part of the meaning of a word (or sentence) *can always be increased* if one chooses. Sharpness is often achieved at the cost of more words, by a longer explanation. Yet, relevance is not magnification. Technical formulas, such as those of symbolic logic, have a kind of precision achieved by brevity, not amplification, since irrelevant words are pruned away. An artistically sharp-cut verbal sketch of a situation may make clear more effectively those parts of a person's character relevant to the author's interest than can a rambling ten-year diary.

We must keep truth tied to the power of language to reveal relevant pattern rather than tying truth to an unattainable infinity of irrelevant detail. One might assume that a story *could* be told with all details made explicit. This is impossible. The hare could then never catch the tortoise. Billions of molecular details would have to be specified, the story would stop, communication would cease, and truth could not exist in any way known to us now. Problems of round numbers, summaries of sermons, the use of "son" in the sense of "descendant," and so on, take place in a perspective of the nature of language as adequate for truly communicating relevant information — relevant on different levels of magnification.

Can any statement then be true? According to Hordern, as the logic of his position would seem to me to lead him on, the answer must be "No." According to my view of the nature of language, the answer must be "Yes."

I end, not with proof, but with a statement of one component of my personal faith: fruitful discourse in science or theology requires us to believe that *within the contexts* of normal discourse *there are some true statements.* Man *must*, sometimes, *act* as if he believed it — or die.

*The moral code should not be viewed
solely as a mechanical tyrant demanding unreasoned conformity. God has
decreed a generalized order designed
to allow us to live happy, useful
lives in the matrix of society. But
God has also left some built-in flexibility for the maximum profitable degree of cultural, group freedom to set
standards relevant to a particular time
and place. The maximum degree of
individual and group happiness comes
by setting local codes (1) to avoid
harm to people, and (2) to serve
them. The first is law, the second
love.*

9 Why Is There a Moral Code?

TODAY I AM ASKING YOU TO LOOK AT AN OLD PROBLEM: WHY IS
there a moral order? Notice that I did not say, "Is there a moral order?" I am assuming that there *is* a moral order. Why
did God impose on us a sensitivity to morality? Well, we
would not be men if we did not have a moral component in us
— we would be beasts. And we could not be in the image of
God if we did not have a moral component. But even these
two answers do not satisfy me. Perhaps the following illustration will lead to an answer.

I once saw some children who were having a good time
playing croquet. Then someone moved the ball a little with
his foot, pretending that it was fun, letting others know he
was doing it. Then someone else, because it was "fun" and
obviously "clever," did the same thing. This gave those two
an unfair advantage — they were kicking the ball, while according to the rules it had to be hit with a mallet — so others started
kicking, too. Soon they were throwing it and batting it out
of turn. Then there was no more game — there could not be

without rules. So the children who really wanted to play moved on because that game had been replaced by chaos.

The one who had started the fun-cheating did not seem to notice that he had ruined the game, but his vanity was inflated because he had been so "clever" — though he could no longer play either. That game we can compare with life here on earth. Frequently someone fails to keep the rules. He does something "cute," or does something against the moral order, or attacks the Bible; and he thinks that this increases his importance. Actually he is spoiling the life game and social chaos has momentarily resulted. If the game had been continued on the high moral order of its included rules, there would have been a higher level of pleasure — that *integrated* pleasure of playing the game, which is similar to the pleasure of the integration of a symphony orchestra. The expense of such pleasure would have been the keeping of the rules.

Now we come to the question, are these rules eternal? Are they temporal?

We begin to find an answer in Mark 2:27 (Weymouth) where Jesus Himself said, "The sabbath was made for man, not man for the sabbath." That tells us that the Sabbath was to be kept for the sake of man — not because it was an eternal law, a law of heaven. God gave man the law because it was good for him. Man needed the rest and so God prescribed rest through a rule. (That is the way we do with our children. It is good for them to get their sleep, so we make it a rule that they have to go to bed at such and such a time.)

From this, I conclude that the ultimate reason for the laws of the moral order is that they are *good for man* and good for his society as a whole. Some people reject this point of view, saying that we must obey God's laws whether they are good for us or not. They are commands of God and that is all that is relevant, these folk affirm.

Some say that these laws are eternal in the heavens. I argue that the commandment against adultery, at least, must be equated with a human order. Since there is no necessity for it to be ordered in heaven, it must be related to earth and not to eternal angels or to God. It seems clear to me, therefore, that the law was made for the good of man and his society.

Now we look at Galatians 5:14 (Weymouth): "For the entire Law is summed up in the one precept, 'You are to love your neighbor as yourself.'" And in Matthew 22:39 Jesus also said, "Thou shalt love thy neighbor as thyself."

Why is the law fulfilled by loving one's neighbor? Because love seeks the neighbor's good *positively*, whereas the law prevents the neighbor's ill *negatively*. These are opposite sides of the same coin.

One side of the coin says that we are not to injure our neighbor; we are to refrain from doing him ill; we are not to step over into his domain for harm. According to the other side of the coin we are required by God to do our neighbor good positively, to step into his domain for his good. This, then, is the reason the law is fulfilled by love. Notice that it has nothing to do with permanent details of an eternal moral law *as such*. Rather it has to do with the ultimate purpose *behind* the moral order, that is, to maintain society for the good of its members. If we seek to maintain the good of the members of society, we are fulfilling the law.

Galatians 5:18 gives us a similar point of view. "But if ye be led of the Spirit, ye are not under the law." Why are we not under the law if we are led of the Spirit? Because if we walk in the Spirit, we have positive control of our inward states and attitudes. If we walk in the law, we have negative control through the avoidance of bad attitudes inwardly. If we positively control our mental state and our actions arising from this inward mental state, then there will be no negative state to be taken care of. Therefore the law would not be needed. We would not be under the law. It would not be aimed at us if we were consistently, positively led of the Spirit. Verse 23 implies that there needs to be no *law* concerning goodness — law is designed as a negative control of the bad. Love is the positive doing good to others which eventually reflects on society, and also reflects on one's self.

Galatians 3:24 says, "Wherefore the law was our schoolmaster to bring us unto Christ, that we might be justified by faith." Why do we need a schoolmaster to bring us to Christ? Specifically, how does the law bring us to Christ? For the answer, let us look at an example from linguistics. If we want to learn a language we have never studied before, we have to learn various sentence patterns. Perhaps we can think of a sentence pattern as being made up of a series of empty compartments — a "subject" compartment, and an "object" compartment, and so on. We fill these compartments with the meaningful words we choose for each occasion. If the empty sentence-forms are utilized adequately in context, then the total context plus the words take on total meaning, total communication, but we have to have the pattern into which we can pour the meanings.

I have the feeling that the law is somewhat like this. If a person learns the law, then he has a pattern for social behavior. He has an available structure, ready to be filled with deeds significant for living and communicating with others, and for living and communicating with God. I think that it is in some such way that the law is a schoolmaster bringing us to Christ.

How does this relate to the way we teach our children? Well, to some extent we teach them law. We spank them to help them to acquire a form of honesty. It is an empty form, an empty compartment, a general principle at first, in that it does not have the meaning content that it eventually should have.

On the mission field, when people move from a pagan social order to a Christian social order, we need to be aware of the problem of transition. We tend to say that some rules are eternal in the heavens and must be fulfilled, whereas actually the thing that is eternal in the heavens is not the particular set of rules for a particular society, but that which is eternal is an insistence on activity which is good and lovely and integrated and wholesome.

We should be careful lest in the name of a moral order we, in fact, injure the new believers as individuals by confusing these complementary phases of life and truth. That is what the fifteenth chapter of Acts teaches us. But for a few exceptions, the Holy Spirit did not fasten specific forms on those converts. "Now, therefore, why provoke God, by laying on the necks of these disciples a yoke?" (Acts 15:10, Weymouth).

There are things that we must teach because God requires them, and hence a Christian must do them. But we do not want our children or our converts to think of God as a reasonless tyrant — although He is indeed our ruler. We want them to learn that the commands of God are all meant to us for good, *because He loves us.* We want them to know that what He requires of us, He requires not because He is ruler and more powerful, but rather because He loves us and that it is for our good.

We know the character of God by looking at Jesus Christ. What we see of the character of Jesus Christ we know to be true of the Father. We never have seen Jesus acting like a tyrant, demanding homage. He was meek and mild and had no jealousy or envy of worship. Jesus Christ, the meekest of all, requires those things of us because they are good for us. For that same reason He built into our genetic equipment a generalized response to a moral order. When we learn to operate within that moral order, as taught us by Jesus Christ and through the Scriptures, then we will be ready to live abundantly (John 10:10). But life abundant can only be had within a system; it cannot be in a vacuum. An abundant life has to be played in terms of a symphony with its integrated chords, its counterpoint. It has to have its melodies and its harmonies. All this requires rules which hold us into a uniform, operating, total harmonious society into which God has come and in which He became incarnate. That is why He came. It was not to bind us with the chains of arbitrary eternal moral rules. The rules which He gives us He teaches us because without them we cannot have a happy integrated game.

If we can understand this, it may free us from the frenzied care as to whether or not we have kept some particular detail of life's ritual. We may be free from worry about details as such and can be vigorously happy as we try to do good for others, knowing that if we are trying to do what is right, unselfishly, we do not have to worry about overlooking some legal detail.

We should teach new converts to be concerned that they do what is good and right and helpful. This does not free them from the requirements of detailed honesty, of carefulness of others in the home, and of faithfulness in the home. That is a part of the rules that are required for the good of society — the best kind of society.

Perhaps it can all be summarized by Deuteronomy 10:12, 13, "And now, Israel, what doth the Lord thy God require of thee, but to fear the Lord thy God, to walk in all his ways, and to love him, and to serve the Lord thy God with all thy heart and with all thy soul, to keep the commandments of the Lord, and his statutes, which I command thee this day *for thy good?*" That is why there is a moral code.   Laws were made for man, not man for laws.

Although the laws of cause and effect point toward determinism as an explanation of our acts, we, nevertheless, accept causality as coming from the hand of God, created and controlled by Him — with His power, love, and mercy as necessary for our responsibility.

10 Cause and Effect in the Christian Life

AS THE SUN RISES AND SETS, AS WE LIVE AND DIE, SO THE LAWS OF cause and effect are rigid.

These laws bind us. If we are lazy, we reap the rewards of laziness. If we are fearful and allow this fear to affect our activities, we will reap the effect of our fearfulness. "Be not deceived; God is not mocked: for whatsoever a man soweth, that shall he also reap" (Galatians 6:7).

If we are unbelieving, not trusting in God, eventually this, too, will catch up with us. Laws of cause and effect lead us to reap what we sow.

The most important thing we are sowing is character. Since we cannot operate without character, what we do reveals its nature and our outlook on the world. Every statement we make, every action we carry out, leaves a slight impression in the brain. It is built into our brain, and our brain builds it into our character, builds it into our soul, and it becomes our essential nature. We become what we do. We reap what we sow, and there is no escape.

In the past I have found it difficult to reconcile this seemingly impersonal, blind cause-and-effect with the fact that God judges. Why does He have to judge us if cause-and-effect is taking care of it?

We see this problem from a different perspective when we study the life of Pharaoh. According to the record, God hardened Pharaoh's heart (Exodus 9:12; 10:20, 27; 11:10; 14:8).

Yet it also says that Pharaoh hardened his own heart (Exodus 8:15, 32; 9:34). Which one was it who hardened his heart? If we look at it from the point of view of cause-and-effect, we would say that Pharaoh's activities and choices set his character and thus his heart became hardened. We would say that cause-and-effect operated with no other agent involved. If, however, we look at it from the point of view of Romans 9:17, 18, we would say that God stepped in and did something to Pharaoh. How do we reconcile these two points of view?

During his examination of Jesus, Pilate asked the question, "What is truth?" (John 18:38). Many people have thought of truth as an abstract principle like goodness or beauty or honor; such hold that this abstract principle is in eternal existence some place in the heavens. If there is a center of truth abstracted away from things and people and God, and if there is God, then God would be judged as good or true according to whether or not He measured up to that principle.

The point of view which appeals to me, however — a view taught by some Christian philosophers — is that truth is not an abstract principle. Truth is not something set apart, different from God, and to which God must conform if He is to be "good." Truth is person. Truth does not exist in a principle, but in a person. This point of view, which seems so hard to grasp philosophically, is clearly shown in Jesus Christ's words, "I am the truth" (John 14:6).

What did He mean? He did not say, "I conform to the truth," nor "I believe in the truth." He said, "I am the truth." In this sense truth is in Jesus Christ, in God. God is truth.

Ultimately, the only true view of the world and of phenomena in the world is God's view. To the extent that I conform to some component of His view, I have truth. When I conform to truth, I do not conform to an abstract principle; I conform to the nature of God.

Now let us return to our initial problem: if laws of cause and effect are in operation, why does God give judgment to us as individuals? To this I would answer: because there is really no cause-and-effect. Cause-and-effect, like truth, is not a "thing" which we can grasp and look at. We cannot see it. There is no thing which is "cause" that will affect us.

You may ask, what is there? There is God. He can affect us. He may affect us directly by His Spirit, with the force of a thunderbolt, or He may choose to woo us gently by stirring up our consciences.

But in addition, God affects us by determining that in the universe certain causes shall bring about certain effects. Cause-and-effect is, therefore, the operation of God through normal channels rather than through special channels.

We have our normal way of acting when we drive a car. We can more or less put it in "automatic pilot" while we carry on a conversation, but when an emergency arises, we take conscious personal control. I have a hunch that God has something for which this automatic pilot will serve as an illustration. That is, His routine way of operating is cause-and-effect, and He is in control of it, so that when cause-and-effect affects us, then God is affecting us.

That is what the Apostle Paul means in Galatians when he says, "Do not kid yourself — God is not blind. What you do, you will get paid for." The causes which we have set in operation by our own personal choices will inevitably bring about certain results. But God is involved because God makes cause-and-effect to work. In other words, cause-and-effect, like truth, must ultimately be vested in the person of God.

Let us turn back for a moment to Pharaoh. When God hardened Pharaoh's heart, He may have hardened it through the routine psychological channels of cause-and-effect, some of which were set in motion by Pharaoh himself. Thus, both God and Pharaoh were involved in the hardening of Pharaoh's heart.

That is, what we sow, we will reap; we will receive the wages for what we have done.

But since cause-and-effect is under the personal control of God, He can introduce into the situation other causes than the ones which we ourselves can control. When in faith we come to God for cleansing from the mess we have made of things, and when we ask for power to reverse causes we have set in motion, God sends in other causes by His Holy Spirit. It may be by direct intervention, or by a combination of circumstances which He controls. We can, therefore, be delivered from the wrath to come, because God will add other causes than those that we have initiated.

Coming back, then, to the important matter of sowing character, let us not deceive ourselves. We will reap what we sow in harsh words to one another. Our idle words will affect our character. Every word which is mean or harsh or dirty will leave its imprint upon us until we reap the character which we have thus sown.

And only by the cleansing power of an outside cause — from God who controls cause — can we become clean and happy again.

*Even in matters of personal guidance
the problems of the relationship between outward control and inner
freedom do not leave us untouched.
The man with one talent failed to see
that guidance through general orders
often carries with it the need for
courage to risk using judgment to
implement them.*

11 Man or Robot

WHAT IS THE DIFFERENCE BETWEEN A MAN AND A ROBOT? FOR
some jobs a robot is more efficient than a man: it is more con-
sistent, and it is more faithful. Routine jobs of a rigorously
repetitive type may in some instances be done by a robot more
efficiently, accurately, and rapidly than can be done by a
man. The man, however, has an enormously greater set of al-
ternatives in living, working, singing, painting, writing, and
in talking to others or to himself than does any robot. It is
this last point that draws the attention of a linguistic analyst,
since the study of language is his province. Then, too, some
anthropologists feel, as professionals, that language ability is
the chief observable difference between a man and a dog or
other animal.

But the difference language makes between man and robot is
not merely the difference between a "thing" with and without
a dictionary — even a robot can be fed spools of tape recordings
to play back words. Man through his spoken or thought language can set up alternative hypotheses and choose between
them. Through language much of his daily judgment operates;
and because of language, a set of ideals, values, morals, and
views of right and wrong can be part of him. Judgment of a
high type requires such a moral base, and man's moral base
requires language. It is exercise of choice in reference to a
set of values for which he himself is morally responsible that
differentiates man most sharply from a robot. Is this potential

for initiative, judgment, and choice desirable? God apparently thought so, because He created man that way. In relation to spiritual life, however, many of us have forgotten that God gave man initiative, and prefer that man act like a high-performance robot. That is, sometimes we wish that we did not have to make a judgment, but prefer that God would decide all details for us by direct, conscious guidance. We prefer this to be so in order that we may not have to take any initiative at all.

If our attitude is of this type — whether tacit or explicit — it perhaps comes from several sources. First, we read again and again in the Old Testament of instances in which the prophets were given direct, verbal instructions as to word and act. Much of the highest guidance of God under the old covenant was of this type. It continued so into the transition era as God led His people from the old to the new. Peter had this type of guidance to reach Cornelius (but evidently then had to figure out for himself, as a Christian filled with the Holy Spirit, what to do next; cf. Acts 10:29, 34, 47; 11:4, 11, 16-18). Paul had it in his conversion, and in a vision of the help needed in Macedonia (but in heading for Bithynia and Troas, and in details of his message at Mars' Hill and at Corinth, in rejecting Mark but choosing Silas and Timothy, he had unpointed pathways to select; cf. Acts 16:7, 8; 17:22-31; I Corinthians 2:2; Acts 15:38, 40; 16:2-3).

A second source of our attitude in which explicit guidance is given such high priority is fear of leaning on our "own understanding" (Proverbs 3:5) lest we stray out of the way. We well know that a fundamental trust in oneself, of the type which leads to being "wise" in one's "own conceit," shuts the gates to effective trust in God and to the receiving of wisdom and power from God. Our ultimate trust must be in God alone (cf. Proverbs 26:12) but we may fail, on the other hand, to sense that trust in God may include trust in His wisdom which made us men — created us to be able to choose and to enjoy choice as being fully men, and to learn by choice. We may fear, thirdly, that when the Word says "it is not in man that walketh to direct his steps" (Jeremiah 10:23) that this eliminates personal judgment, if we are to claim the promise that "he shall direct thy paths" (Proverbs 3:6).

As a result of such convictions and fears we may be tempted to believe that a person of the highest spiritual maturity *always* obtains direct guidance for both important and unimportant decisions. In the first blush of growing spirit, a youth may find great blessing in direct guidance as to small matters — where to go, whom to see, what to say, what to wear, and an infinity of small items. God teaches through these, and by them may help to guide to thrilling blessing.

Yet, in time, these very blessings — looked at and desired for their own sake, as spiritual — may lead to a snare. They can bring a person into a swamp of subjectivism which is vacillating, unstable, and a source of despair. One may set up as a principle of guidance the necessity of receiving a psychological impression (sometimes falsely labelled as a "trying of the spirits"). This can lead to unwise, impractical actions in the name of God — I have seen people leave the mission field for precisely this reason. Such an extreme attitude can also lead to spiritual paralysis in which we refuse to act at all unless such subjective impressions of guidance are obtained. We say to ourselves, if we are in this attitude, "If I am not sure of God's will (by subjective tests of the will of the Holy Spirit) I will not move at all."

In such a spiritual state we fear more to move and chance a mistake than we fear to refuse to follow general orders for which judgment and initiative are required. The valuable attitude of patient, prayerful, and careful waiting to sift one's motives and to allow issues to become clarified is herein confused with the supposed value of acting only on a basis of subjective, direct guidance. When seeing the evidence pointing to these genuine dangers it is altogether too easy to reach a false conclusion — that guidance, to be based on trust in God, must come only through an impression direct on our spirits. We are prone to forget the scriptural statements which show that guidance may be *through the Word*, which is a light to the road which may otherwise be dark (Psalm 119:105), and that moral standards, used, give guidance, since *"the integrity of the upright shall guide them"* (Proverbs 11:3), and *"the righteousness of the perfect shall direct his way"* (Proverbs 11:5; cf. also Proverbs 3:23; 6:20-22; 10:9). If someone asks, "Is there not a 'way that seemeth right to man, but the end thereof are the ways of death'?" (Proverbs 14:12), the answer is clearly "Yes." But the contexts throughout Proverbs show that this way is the way of the one who rejects God — not the way of the one walking in righteousness (Proverbs 1:29-30; 2:12-15). In this extreme position we have ultimately desired to be a kind of robot rather than man. We have wanted to escape the responsibility which God is training us up to carry. Spiritually we have ceased to have that maturity of judgment which leads to *walking* in righteousness.

The mature spiritual life, in my view, is a *balanced life* — and needs to include components both of direct guidance and of guidance through judgment. Since direct guidance has received much emphasis, I would like to direct the remainder of this article to the balancing truth — the need for initiative and the use of judgment.

Now, in reference to this problem, let us look at a parable: "A certain nobleman went into a far country, to receive for himself a kingdom, and to return. And he called ten servants of his, and gave them ten pounds" (Luke 19:12, 13, ARV). And he said to them, "Trade with these until I come" (Luke 19:13, Montgomery). With that admonition to get busy, and the sweeping indication as to their goal and technique (trading), he left them.

The men knew what a trader was supposed to do. He bought something and planned how he could sell it for more. Sometimes he might gain, and occasionally he might lose, but gradually by trading back and forth he would expect to build up a profit. Some of the ten servants immediately got to work, buying and selling with the money he had given them. But one of them simply put the money in a hiding place and kept it safely. When the nobleman returned, one of his servants came to him and said, "Master, your pound has made ten pounds." And the nobleman said, "Well done. . . . Because you have been found faithful in a very little, have authority over ten cities" (Luke 19:16, 17, Montgomery).

Notice that "faithful" here means that he was faithful in exercising God-given judgment and *God-ordered initiative*.

Observe, also, that the reward of the men who used their abilities and capital was neither money, nor honor — but *au-*

thority. It was opportunity for judgment — an opening for use of increased initiative and responsibility therein.

Then, according to the parable, another servant came and said, "Here, Master, is your pound which I was keeping safe in a napkin. For I was afraid of you, because you are a hard man" (Luke 19:20, 21, Montgomery). Of what was he afraid? He was afraid to take initiative. He had been given general orders to trade, but he did not have detailed guidance, and he was afraid of trusting his judgment in what to buy and how to sell. He was afraid even though he was presumably competent.

But this servant, afraid to take responsibility, had done nothing, so the Master said to him, in effect, "Why you miserable servant! You wicked slave" (cf. Luke 19:22, Montgomery). In what respect was the servant wicked? He had not stolen; he had not cheated. The only thing he had done wrong was to sit when he had been given a general command which indicated the type of work he should do. He had refused to act like a man, refused to use judgment for the details of the work. Instead, he had tried to act like a robot, hiding refusal to work under the excuse that he had not gotten specific guidance for all the details of the work he was supposed to know. As a result, he was rated as wicked — immoral! We may compare this judgment with the one in Proverbs 18:9: "He that is slack in his work is brother to him that is a destroyer." The person without drive is morally related to a person who, in a desire to avoid work and in anger at his employer, smashes property with a sledge hammer.

This servant later may have tried to justify himself to his colleagues by saying that he was "afraid of making a mistake." But in trying to avoid a "mistake," by refusing to make any positive decisions at all, the servant gained nothing since his Master became disgusted anyway.

I personally think that if he had tried, however, but had lost his pound, he could have gone to the Master and said, "Master, you told me to trade — so I did my best. But I sure made a mess of it. I am awfully sorry I was so stupid." I think the Master would then have said to him, "You had a bad time, did you? Well, if I give you another chance, do you

think you can do better next time?   Here — take this, and
try again.   Charge the first pound up to education."
     Instead, the Master's reaction to his reasoning was, "Take
from him the pound, and give it to him who hath ten pounds"
(Luke 19:24).   We see here that not only was the servant
judged to be immoral and lazy when he refused to take responsibility, but that — in direct contrast to the ones who
earned a right to use greater judgment — he lost his opportunity
to exercise as much judgment as he previously had been capable
of.   Probably, too, his capacity for wise judgment was itself
damaged by being unused, and by having its earlier timid
promptings rejected.
     Similar things are true even in physical life.   It seems to be
a law of the universe, built into our physical bodies, that we
either exercise or die.
     In the spiritual realm, too, we need to exercise our faculties.
If we refuse to take spiritual initiative, but wait insistently for
the will of God to be revealed directly when He has already
given us adequate general orders and brains, we may atrophy.
     In the related parable of Matthew 25, the fearful "unprofitable
servant" is cast into the outer darkness.   As a commentary on
the phrase "unprofitable servant" one may turn to Luke 17:4-10.
Here, the servant was expected to go *beyond* routine specific
duty, beyond specific orders, beyond 'reasonable' requirements
of forgiveness of others (verse 4) or of physical labor in field
and home: "Doth he thank that servant because he did the
things that were commanded him? I trow not. So likewise ye,
when ye shall have done all those things which are commanded
you, say, We are unprofitable servants: we have done that
which was our duty to do" (verses 9-10).   Would a housewife
— hiring a cleaning woman to go through her house from top
to bottom in the spring — be happy if she had to say, "Clean
that corner there . . . Now this corner . . . Now that corner. . .
Dust that window sill . . . Now dust that window sill . . . Do
not forget to sweep after you have picked up the rug . . . etc."?
Or would she want to be able to give general instructions which
would last for an hour or two?
     Is not such a servant like a robot?   And does God want us
to grow up like *that* without judgment to be used?   We are
expected to judge issues.   Evidence?   Our rated capacity as

judges in heaven. "Know ye not that we shall judge angels? how much more things that pertain to this life?" (I Corinthians 6:3).

How, then, do these considerations affect our daily lives? What am I going to do this next hour? I do not have a direct revelation from Him about it — I have to decide. Where am I going to put my energies today? I have to decide.

Solomon was told to ask for what he wanted (I Kings 3:5) and he did ask, and was given his request. Do you not suppose that if God considered it good to urge Solomon to choose, and honored that choice, that He sometimes wishes us to do so too? In this freedom God has trusted Christians with general orders through Scripture. Sometimes, however, when unwise or ignorant choices are about to get us into trouble, God graciously steps in, overrules our decisions, and stops us. I think this is the type of freedom that Paul had when he used his initiative to head for Bithynia and was stopped.

Some people talk almost exclusively about being in the "center" of God's will, considering that center as a pinpoint. Perhaps some of our teaching about guidance could be made more helpful if we supplemented it by additional figures of speech. It is useful at times, for example, to think of God's will as an *area* in a television wave guide, or tube. As I understand it, the waves in this tube bounce back and forth anywhere within the tube that they "want" to go, completely free so long as they remain in the tube. They are not channeled to a thin line — they just cannot go outside of the wave guide.

To me this is a picture of the way God wants Christians to live. We are not to be robots, incapable of — or afraid of — taking initiative. We are to be free to think and act within the general orders and principles of character revealed in the Word and impressed on our consciences by the Holy Spirit. We are not to get outside of His will — outside of the "wave guide" — by committing murder, or adultery, or by being unkind, or unhappy, or unfruitful. But as long as we are within the limits of the revealed will of God in the Scriptures, in godliness, and in service to others, we can have anything physically available to us which we desire to choose. Solomon did. The Psalmist could, delighting in Him and receiving the desires of the heart (Psalm 37:4). In the words of the Psalmist, who has taught us this lesson: "Blessed is the man that walketh not in the counsel of the ungodly . . . But his delight is in the law of the Lord . . . *whatsoever* he doeth shall prosper" (Psalm 1:1-3).

If one refuses to view self as needing integration with God and neighbor, one shrivels like a shrub in the desert. From society one gets language, knowledge, stimulus, fellowship, and those environmental factors which help make and keep us human. From God one receives ultimate power for living, as well as immediate strength for building the kind of character which one may want above almost all else on earth. Selfishness breeds death by cutting one off from the resources of communion with man and with God.

12 The Death of Independence

"LET NOT THE WISE MAN GLORY IN HIS WISDOM, LET NOT THE mighty man glory in his might, let not the rich man glory in his riches; but let him who glories glory in this, that he understands and knows me, that I am the Lord who practices kindness, justice, and righteousness in the earth; for in these things I delight, says the Lord" (Jeremiah 9:23, 24).

This idea is repeated in the New Testament: "Let him who boasts, boast of the Lord" (II Corinthians 10:17).

Some questions present themselves as we read these words. Why is it good for us to boast about God but not about ourselves? Why is it good for God to insist that we boast about Him? Is not that selfish of Him? How can it be that we must refuse to boast of ourselves, but God can insist that we boast about Him?

Some reasons for not boasting about ourselves are apparent. For one thing, it is unpleasant and distasteful to hear a person boast about himself, but that still does not mean that it is sin.

Why is it sin to boast about oneself? Or why is pride, which is related to boasting, sin? Why do we not like pride in others?

Although unpleasant, does it not seem harmless? Why should it be forbidden?

Of course, pride is foolish. The Apostle Paul saw that when he said, "But whatever any one dares to boast of — I am speaking as a fool — I also dare to boast of that" (II Corinthians 11:21). Why is pride foolish? For one thing, because a person is not that competent. Nobody is as good as he thinks he is. But why is this proud boasting *sin*?

Why does God resist the proud? Jeremiah 17:5 starts to give us the answer: "Thus says the Lord: Cursed is the man who trusts in man." Notice that this answer implies that boasting in yourself leads to *trusting* in yourself. Nobody can claim repeatedly that he is competent without beginning to believe it. When we claim that we are wise, we soon believe that we are wise, and then we trust in ourselves as wise and competent. Thus boasting in myself leads me to trust in myself, and trusting in myself turns me away from trusting in the Lord. Of such a person the Lord says, "He is like a shrub in the desert, and shall not see any good come. He shall dwell in the parched places of the wilderness, in an uninhabited salt land" (Jeremiah 17:5).

The interpretation is quite clear. A shrub in the desert has no water. It is parched and shriveled. A shrub in the desert may appear to be partly independent, but because of its independence it fails to get from the outside that which it needs to sustain luxurious growth; and even a shrub in the desert can survive only by water from outside itself.

When a person boasts of himself, trusts in himself and turns away from trusting in God, he closes the gates to adequate sustenance and health from God. In other words, boasting leads to independence, and independence is the great sin because it leads to ruin. In the garden of Eden (Genesis 3:5) the serpent said to the woman, "You will be like God" — that is, independent.

Why should a person not want to be independent? Because if a person succeeds in becoming independent, he dies. If the environment is removed, if the air is removed, if the water is removed, he cannot live. He has no sustenance within himself to last more than a fraction of a minute.

Independence is death because independence cuts off the source of supply. God upholds the universe and gives it power, and the only person who can survive is one who is held up by the power of God.

Now notice the man who chooses to be dependent. He is described in the verses which immediately follow those describing the shrub: "Blessed is the man who trusts in the Lord, whose trust is the Lord. He is like a tree planted by water, that sends out its roots by the stream, and does not fear when heat comes, for its leaves remain green, and is not anxious in the year of drought, for it does not cease to bear fruit" (Jeremiah 17:7, 8).

The only tree which can bear fruit is one that seeks with its roots for water and sustenance outside itself. Similarly, the only man who can bear fruit is one who trusts in God and looks to Him for character.

If a man chooses to be independent, he may. He has free will; he may choose independence — and die. But if he wants fruit, if he wants strength, if he wants power, if he wants to work, he must be geared into the universe, to God who made it, and to his fellow men.

Some of us agree more easily to dependence upon God than we do to dependence upon our fellow men, but in society the only ones who can survive as normal men are those who can communicate with others. People who cut themselves off and reject interaction with others cannot serve others or live happy, full lives according to their basic nature.

To change the figure of speech, consider your wrist watch. It has wheels. Suppose every wheel were self-conscious and wanted to be independent. And suppose one of the wheels said, "I am tired of being kicked in the teeth! I will be independent. I will unhook myself from my environment and be *me*. I will turn when I choose and I will refuse to turn when someone kicks me around."

But soon after it is unhooked, the wheel coasts to a halt. It has achieved independence, but at the expense of life. It no longer tells time nor serves man.

Like the wheels of that watch, we must be geared into God and into our environment if we are to serve Him and serve our fellows. Sometimes we dislike being held back by others, even other Christians. We want to be free to do as we think is wise, but a wheel that is not held back loses its strength, its drive. Independence is achieved, but power through tension is lost.

God has allowed us independence if we want it. Lots of people do want it, and they get it. But what do they get with it? Selfishness and egocentricity. And selfishness leads to corrosion of personality because it isolates. And isolation is the road to hell.

Such a road is characterized by annoyance at the interference of others who control us and hold us in, who check our independence.

Ultimately the only way off the road is through giving up independence at the offer of slavery. Christ says, "Come and be my slave. Take my yoke and become free" (see Matthew 11:28-30).

But if submission to Him as Lord is rejected, we will have made a basic choice, and we will reap what we have chosen. We will receive what we have demanded. God would have to take back His gift of free will to reach us, and this He will not do lest He wreck creation.

From this desire for independence — this pride of life — proceeds all that hurts us and wrecks the lives of others.

Now the opposite of independence is integration. Integration in marriage is a merging of lives, service and work. Integration in society as a whole is a merging of effort, will and power. Integration in service for God involves surrender to God. Lack of such surrender — independence — is sin, stifling service and paralyzing any sense of joy through fellowship with others.

But we have not yet answered our question about God: why is it not wrong for God to ask us to boast of Him?

It is not wrong because He is the heart, the source of any vertical or horizontal integration, and everything must be geared into Him to work effectively.

He alone is the Independent One.

It does us no harm to be proud of our God — rather it leads to a recognition of our dependence on Him and our gearing into His power. It is not selfishness on His part to demand it of us — rather it is part of His service to us. And it is a recognition of truth, of reality.

In serving Him, we are allowed to be integrated with Him who is the source of power and the source of life.

The parts of a sonnet, or crucial components of a sentence type, may be planned or determined from the beginning. Some day, in retrospect, we will see our life as God sees it — as a total which is also planned. And we will see that it is good.

13 All in All: A Linguistic Parable

WHEN GOD CREATES A SEED, HE KNOWS HOW IT WILL GROW. Its beginning and development are all in the seed. The seed plus life is, in a small sense, an all in all.

God has built the universe like a seed. In a similar sense it is an all in all, and God controls it, holds it, builds it, and knows what will come out of it. "And he is before all things [referring to Christ] and by him all things consist" (Colossians 1:17). "And when all things shall be subdued unto him, then shall the Son also himself be subject unto him that put all things under him, that God may be all in all" (I Corinthians 15:28).

Because God is all in all, there is a unity in every work. We should, therefore, be looking in our everyday tasks for new parables that will teach us about God. The person whose life is given to washing dishes should find parables in the dishes. So should the engineer, the medical researcher, the secretary.

My field is linguistics. I therefore look for linguistic parables.

God is all in all from the beginning to the end, from birth to death, from morning until it is time to sleep. From the beginning of the universe to its end.

Note the linguistic illustration in Revelation 1:8. Jesus Christ says, "I am Alpha and Omega," I am all from A to Z, everything "which is, and which was, and which is to come." This is an illustration of all in all.

In linguistics I see other illustrations of patterns which imply a whole. If someone starts a sentence, "Tomorrow I have to —" we know that something more will be said to finish it. The missing part might be "go downtown" or "finish my term paper," but we cannot make sense out of that sentence until it is finished. It is a whole.

Similarly, a poem is not just a collection of words. It must have rhyme, meter, or whatever structural characteristics go with the kind of verse being created. Before anyone can begin writing a poem, he has to know something of the end, if the poetic structure is to be true to pattern.

Now, then, if a person cannot write a sonnet without knowing the pattern of the end before he writes the beginning, can we suppose that God will shape a character without knowing the end from the beginning?

Some poems are intricate. The first line does not have much to do with the second line, nor the second with the third. It is the fourth or fifth line that rhymes with the first. The pattern is too involved, too long, too faint to see the end from the beginning, unless you know the plan.

Similarly, God has a plan that is part of His all in all. That plan has layers in it. There is a spiritual layer, and a physical layer — health, sickness, money, economics. The activities of one layer affect the others. For example, if I stay up until three A.M., I may be so tired the next day that I have spiritual problems. We are not just flesh and blood. We are wholes.

Our lives are planned as a whole, but we may be ignorant of part of the plan, and that ignorance is a great trial to us. We want to understand everything about our growth from the beginning to the end, and we may feel a bit resentful if something about it does not strike us as sensible. Just as the beginning of a sentence is not useful to us until we have the end, so we cannot understand fully the beginning of God's plan for our lives until we know the end. Perhaps we do not understand a certain section because its relevance does not come from the beginning but from the end, which we cannot see.

If we ask, Why has God not revealed the end to us? I think linguistics shows part of the reason. We cannot teach a two-year-old to understand *Paradise Lost* for linguistic reasons: he has not learned the language.

God has a "language" that we must learn. A lot of it is written in struggle. Part of it is written in tears. Some of it we learn only when we are hurt in such a way that we know how to avoid hurting someone else. Part of that language can be learned only through pain, and so we have pain.

The Scriptures tell us that it is impossible for us to understand everything now, but they promise that someday we will understand. To me that is a very precious promise — I would *like* to understand. Eventually we will know. "For now we see in a mirror dimly, but then face to face. Now I know in part; then I shall understand fully, even as I have been fully understood" (I Corinthians 13:12). Does this mean that I am to know my program as God knows it? In some sense, yes. Am I to understand my part in the universe as God understands it? Yes. Am I to understand my problems and disappointments as God understands them? Yes. I am to know fully, just as fully as God knows me — in some sense.

This does not mean that I will know the number of hairs on my head, even though God knows (Matthew 10:30). It does not mean that I will know how many corpuscles I have in my blood stream. That kind of knowledge might not be structurally relevant to us in heaven. To know "even as I have been fully understood" is different — something more powerful, more wonderful. I think it means that we will understand the plan of our lives and the purpose behind it. The meaning of the universe will be clear to us, as well as our personal involvement in that meaning.

The Lord Jesus told His disciples, "I have yet many things to say unto you, but ye cannot bear them now" (John 16:12). Even He, in the days of His flesh and blood, could not tell His disciples some of the things He wanted them to know. They were not ready.

And there are some things He wants us to know, but we cannot understand them because we are not ready. One of these days we will be ready. We will have learned the "language." Then we will see that God's plan for our lives has been good. God is all in all. And in the same way that He is integrated, He has chosen that we be integrated.

He has planned everything from A to Z. It is all one. It all interpenetrates. It all makes sense. — Even my failures have been woven into the pattern. In some languages, we note, two negatives can be used by the craftsman to make a positive.

PART III: COMMITMENT

The commitment to individual faith seldom comes through a simple train of logical thought, or as one of uncomplicated acceptance or rebellion. In my own case, a Christian home, intellectual struggles with science, and a burning thirst for character acceptable to God led in mature life to renewed trust in God as a source of power for character and intellectual work.

14 Why I Believe in God

ALL OF US PICK UP — PERHAPS IN GARBLED FORM — SOME OF THE ideas of the intellectual climate in which we live.

One idea which seems to be drifting around from some psychiatric sources is that a man who has a guilt complex has not sinned. The psychiatrist says, "You may be maladjusted, you may have a personality which needs a bit of modification, but you have not sinned."

But God says, "Behold, I will enter into judgment with thee, because thou sayest, 'I have not sinned'" (Jeremiah 2:35).

Another contemporary idea, in this instance probably springing from the intellectual climate of anthropology, is the implication that we have different customs but we really have not sinned, and do not need to blush. But this idea again is contrary to God's Word: "Were they ashamed when they had committed abomination? Nay, they were not at all ashamed, neither could they blush" (Jeremiah 8:12).

The climate in which I grew up was quite different, for mine was a Christian home. My first religious memories are of my mother as she sang in family prayers, "Saviour, like a Shepherd lead us," and "There were ninety and nine that safely lay in the shelter of the fold." In such a climate I grew up serving my acknowledged Lord. But "sin" as a generalized concept was not given much thought.

It was years after I had been a Christian, years after I had

83

been a Bible translator, that I woke up to the realization that I was a sinner in a manner that I had not previously understood. That realization came to me when I was rebuked for being unkind and unnecessarily sharp.

It happened when I was trying to lead a man to Christ — or save him for Christ at a time when he was in danger of leaving the road to discipleship. I had taken what I thought was an effective method for jolting him into seeing the danger of his actions. When I had finished, a saint of God called James 3:17 to my attention: "But the wisdom from above is first pure, then peaceable, gentle. . . ."

I was a member of the board of Wycliffe Bible Translators, supposedly because I had a certain measure of wisdom. But I was not gentle. And the Word of God drove home the fact that "if your wisdom is not gentle, it is not from above."

That rocked me to the core.

I had never been so deeply rocked, and I hope I never will be again.

I started to study the Word of God to see what this new idea meant in relation to me. I found in Galatians 5:22 that "the fruit of the Spirit is love, joy, peace, longsuffering, gentleness. . . ." I did not have gentleness. There was nothing hidden about the fact — all my colleagues knew I did not have it.

I said to myself, "I am responsible to be gentle and kindly." I read carefully the places where the results of the working of the Spirit of God are listed, but nowhere did it say, "He writes linguistic textbooks." I could not even find that it said, "He translates the Bible." Linguistics was not listed there, nor drive, nor energy, nor initiative. It said "joy," but I did not have it consistently; it said "peace," but I was often upset; "gentleness," but I was tough.

I took Galatians 5:22 and 23 as a measuring stick, put it alongside my character and found that I did not even register on the scale.

I looked at some of my colleagues in Mexico, and many of them measured up well. They were gentle and liked people. I did not. They were kindly. I was not. — When I saw this I became angry. I said, "Lord, I have worked years, I have hazarded my life, I have hazarded my health again and again for You. And I am not even on the scale."

I did not have to wait until I arrived in heaven to see something of what it means that "the first shall be last." Already I was seeing it in the Word of God. I said, "It is not fair." I came as close as I dared to swearing at Him to His face. I said, "If that is the way things line up, You can have your heaven."

But God had hold of me, and so, because of His grace, I did not quite mean it. I surrendered to His will and His Spirit. Then, with His help and His continued pressure, began the struggle of changing my life in order to improve my grade on His scale.

In the past I had occasionally been much annoyed at linguistics students who, because they could not make an A, refused to work even to get a C. False pride led them to fail to do their best, and Luke 19:22 condemned them. But now the shoe was on the other foot. I obviously could not, even with severe effort, make an A in personal graciousness, and I was therefore tempted not to try. But when this analogy struck me, I surrendered to fuller depths and prayed, "Lord, help me at least to work up to a C and not to shrink from the struggle because of pride."

He was ready to help, and since the fruits of the Spirit are a gift from Him, I began to pray every morning, "Lord, give me joy." Well, that helped for a few hours, but by the next morning I did not have it spontaneously and without reserve. I prayed that prayer every day, and many times a day. After six months or so I was a little bit happy when I woke up.

Well, I said, this is wonderful! I will try another one on the list. (I skipped over "love" because I could not get close enough to that one even to begin working on it.) So I took "gentleness."

One day I would be all right, and even the next day — then someone would surprise me and I would clobber him with words. Well, I got about three weeks into gentleness but by then I was gloomy again. I said, "Lord, I have slipped." So I quit trying first of all for gentleness and went back to work on joy.

I have not yet been able to get the whole way through that list in Galatians 5:22 and 23. So some day if you see me cruel and harsh, just say, "There goes Ken Pike. That is the way he really is." And you will be telling the truth.

Then if you should happen to see me kindly when you did not expect it, just say, "Well, the Lord must have worked him into line this morning." And that will be true, too.

But, curiously enough, gentleness is not what I am writing about. My topic is far different. What I have just said is simply laying the background for what I have to say.

What I really want to say is that this is the way the Lord prepared me for an intellectual battle that came later on. The experience I have just described served as the background.

You see, I am an intellectual, or am supposed to be, and as such I have the temptations of those peculiar creatures. Some time ago all the temptations of an intellectual suddenly started to come at me. Many things that I thought I knew partially disintegrated when I tried to see the solidity behind the Word of God. What made it solid? History. The resurrection of Jesus Christ is the best attested fact in history, I had always said.

But I began to meet people who objected: "You know perfectly well that people see things according to their background and personal experience. The disciples were telling the truth as they saw it, perhaps, but this is no assurance that if we had been there we would have seen the same thing that they saw." And I had to admit that what they said had enough truth in it to make impossible an argument which would be compelling to the unbeliever.

When the validity of the Bible was questioned, I debated within myself: Although I really believe these Scriptures to be the documents they claim to be, can we *prove* it intellectually? And in spite of having read books setting out to do that very thing, I for one had to admit that I did not know how to prove the certainty of Bible truth to those who did not acknowledge the validity of Christianity.

I was bothered, too, when I began to hear about carbon-14 dating. And I very carefully read everything available to me that had been published on the topic up to that time. I saw how this method of dating was affecting some of the cultural dates that had been set previously. This forced me to expand more explicitly the dates of cultural history into time depths further than I had wished to admit even to myself.

Then the question of anthropology came along, and as I read the writings of cultural determinists, I began to realize that to some extent they had seen a phase of truth. And it seemed to me, although they themselves might not know it, that their view might somehow be related to the fact that we are dead — "totally conditioned" by — trespasses and sins (Ephesians 2:1; compare also Jeremiah 13:23, "Can the Ethiopian change his skin, or the leopard his spots? Then may ye also do good, that are accustomed to do evil.") And I said, How do I answer them?

I had no compelling argument which would reach the unconvinced scholars in the university. On the contrary, I felt less confidence in the effectiveness of Christian apologetics for such purposes.

Then I took a brief glance at some philosophy, and I was shocked when I first read a book that took it for granted that there was no design in the universe. This to me was appalling. As I read more of this literature, and as I read biological literature, the argument that design in the universe *proved* the existence of God no longer seemed to me as useful as I had thought for witnessing to others — or in supporting my own personal belief in Christianity.

Part of my difficulty — I now see in retrospect — seems to have been that I had always thought of design in nature (as in a wrist watch) to be tied to fiat creation. Fiat design would have been completely visible — so I naively assumed — at the completion of the initial creation. It seemed to me, in general, that this was the way the scientists interpreted the evangelical's argument from design. Both their feelings and mine seemed to be based on proclamations of evangelicals who were not scientists. Perhaps we should all have known better, perhaps we should have consulted more scholarly evangelical writings. Be that as it may, fiat design, completed ages before we could find evidence for any history of the process by which it was brought to completion, was what I had assumed to be the evangelical position.

Specifically, for instance, I had heard arguments — which were strongly convincing to me — based upon the mutual dependence of certain kinds of bugs. One bug lived only by killing the other particular kind, planting its own offspring in it, and having the young grow by eating the other for food, etc. Such specificity — the argument was presented to me — could come only from design, not from chance — and the design proved fiat creation, with the bug relation surviving from earliest times.

But I suddenly found this argument disintegrating, for me, when I began to sense the strength of evidence of the numbers of sharply different kinds of related animals, each thus closely geared into its environment. When I visited Australia, I was told that two hundred kinds of kangaroos, more or less, were on that continent. Many I saw in their zoo. Some lived in rocks, others on the deserts. The rat kangaroo was tiny. One relative in New Guinea climbed trees. Other more distantly related pouch-bearing animals (the koala bear) climbed trees in Australia. One was like a wild, vicious fox, or dog, and so on. Surely there were not two hundred such varieties in the ark, to put it bluntly, since there could not be physical room for all these and other similarly differentiated animal families. Yet — and here the pinch came — many of these were obviously geared to their environment; there seemed to me to be as much evidence for fiat, immediate creation here as in other instances which I had heard used as evidence of such creation. What, then, must be the impact of such evidence on an argument for fiat total design, completely executed at the dawn of the world?

This problem was accentuated from two other sources which blurred for me the lines between species more than could be admitted without destroying the apologetic arguments which I had read — and accepted uncritically — as a teen-ager. The first was that, within the laboratory, varieties of miscroscopic organisms were being developed with extraordinary adaptive characteristics. From a common batch, half could be taken, and have a poison mixed with their liquid environment. Most of these died, but eventually a strain developed which not only grew well in the poison, but died if the "poison" — now an essential — were removed. Descendants of the original type, not accustomed to that poison, still died on contact.

This situation deals only with minor varieties. The next which affected me deals with the basic source of our understanding of the line of demarcation between species as such.

I have two friends who are among those scientists who determine what the various species of fish are. They take a fish
that has never been seen before and they classify it. One of
the men is jokingly called a "joiner," and the other a "splitter."
If the "joiner" finds a fish that is on the border line between
two recognized species, he is likely to say: "Why make a separate species out of it?" — and put it into a class along with one
of the other species.

The "splitter" likes everything to be clean cut, so when he
finds a fish that is on the border line he is more likely to say:
"Let's make a separate species out of it" — and put it into a
separate class. In that sense they "make" the species — or the
classification of species. To me it was a shocking thing that
the boundaries of a species could be set, so far as science is
concerned, by men. It bothered me when I thought of this in
relation to "design in the universe" as long as I thought of that
design as tied to unchanging and sharply delineated species.

And how could the scientist be persuaded to accept an argument for design in the universe, if that argument were keyed
into a conviction of the unchanging character of species, that
is, into a classification of the species which in fact changed at
the borders whenever he or his colleagues changed their minds?
How could they be expected to respond to an argument from
design if that argument were tied inextricably to an assumption
that design was executed by fiat, without some slow development and outworking? How could they accept that argument, if they found evidence in their laboratories of adaption
of a kind which appeared to them completely analogous to those
instances which are used elsewhere as evidence of God's fiat
design, a design which was supposedly completely executed before the beginning of history?

My own solution to this particular problem was to conclude
that the term "design" must be extended further[1] than I had

1. I believe, of course, in the book of Genesis. The precise interpretation
which will ultimately best fit the observed data to this revelation has not
yet been worked out for us by the evangelical theologians in a way which
leads them to a firm, unanimous judgment. Until they can get further
along with this general task for the church as a whole, my own personal
judgment tentatively operates within the general area of the principle summarized by Bernard Ramm under the phrase "progressive creation" in his

supposed when I was growing up. Design must be seen in some instances as coming from God, even though it appeared as the result of God's laws working in historical time. This, however, did not take care of the deeper problem as to proof of the presence of design or the existence of God. Though I personally continued to believe that design is present, I still did not see that it *compelled* men to believe; obviously many of my university colleagues had not believed. Why not? Could they not see it? Is, or is not, this design "visible" in the sense that Christian apologetic literature implies? Is, or is not, a person morally guilty who refuses to deduce from seeing nature that God has designed it?

For many years I had felt the weight of Romans 1:20 which says that the "eternal power and Godhead" of the Lord have been revealed to man — clearly — in nature, so that they are

book, *The Christian View of Science and Scripture* (Eerdmans, Grand Rapids, 1954) pp. 112-17, 227-28, 271-93. For now, at least, it appears to me that this view leaves adequate room for the evidence of observable change within species while affirming the essential fact of God as Creator. Note Ramm's differentiation between progressive creation (which he accepts) and theistic evolution (which he rejects, as do I): "From time to time the great creative acts, *de novo*, took place . . . This is not theistic evolution which calls for creation from within with no acts *de novo*. It is progressive creationism . . . We agree with Gedney that the geological record does not reveal a continuity, an evolution, but that it reveals great gaps. Animal forms appear suddenly. The geologist writes: 'form X appeared in the Devonian.' The theologian informs him that from the theological vantage point the word *appeared* is to be rendered *created*" (p. 228). "We believe in several acts of fiat creation in the history of the earth, and this clearly differentiates this view from theistic evolution" (p. 116).

For a discussion of the degree to which the current evangelical movement insists that we must accept change within species, see the series of articles entitled "The Story of Creation" which appeared in *Christian Life* in March, September, 1955; January, May, 1956. Contributors or consultants included such men as James O. Buswell, III, Irving W. Knobloch, Russell Mixter, Kenneth S. Kantzer (Wheaton College), R. Laird Harris (Covenant Theological Seminary), Irvin A. Wills (John Brown University), Gleason L. Archer (Fuller Theological Seminary), John W. Klotz (Concordia College), R. S. Beal (Conservative Baptist Theological Seminary). Note the following: "To be realistic about it, scientists, theologians and laymen must all admit that nature indicates change or transformism and the Bible does not teach the 'fixity of the species'" (p. 11). Also "the big problem comes in deciding how far down or up the biological ladder this diversification goes" (p. 11).

"without excuse." Because of this Scriptural statement, I now insisted to myself, we must conclude that man is morally responsible for seeing in nature that there is a God. Yet in spite of this conclusion the evidence clearly included the fact that many scientists profess *not* to see through nature any evidence for the existence of God. How could I reconcile this difference so that the explanation would satisfy me at least — even though it might not be convincing to others?

I came to the conclusion that in heaven, at the judgment seat, God will hold all men responsible for their basic philosophical assumptions, and that this choice of an epistemology is a *moral* choice. It seemed to me that it *must* be a moral issue — else how can God judge the world? This follows, I felt, since it appears that once a person is committed to a basic world view, a particular "proof" is valid, and arguments are compelling, only within his chosen system of belief; items which disagree with that view cannot be consistently entertained.

People cannot be convinced if they choose not to be. How, then, can they be held to be morally guilty for failing to believe something which is nonsense within their philosophical framework? I could reach this conclusion, I saw, only by building on the assumption — unprovable by man — that an epistemological choice is a moral one. It seemed to me that some kinds' of unbelief can be proved to be morally wrong only if the philosophical system leading to it can be demonstrated to be morally wrong. But God, I firmly believe, will be able to point out to every man the very moment or period when, years before, he took the crucial step toward choosing an inadequate philosophical base or system as a cloak to hide his moral responsibility.

Yet I still was not satisfied. How could scholars get into such a state? From the viewpoint of the first chapter of Romans, they do so by "professing themselves to be wise." That is, because of pride of independence they choose a philosophical system which does not leave room for the God and Father of our Lord Jesus Christ. Thus they become "fools" since they thereby abandon one of the basic assumptions essential for obtaining an understanding of truth about the world.

Fear of the Lord is the beginning — and basic assumption — of wisdom in that it sets up the only ultimately adequate epistemological starting point. As fools epistemologically, "their foolish heart is darkened" and their assumptions *do not allow* them to *see* design. They have "changed the truth of God" for "a lie." That is, they have chosen to believe in a developmentalism divorced from God's purpose. It is at this point that "proofs" of the existence of God are of little effect. A philosophical system can be impervious to all such arguments. I was troubled by these matters when I tried to talk to my colleagues on the Michigan faculty. I realized that Christian claims about eternity were in sharp clash with their assumption. When I affirmed that God is Ruler, that Christ is Master, and that the Bible is the Word of God, I found no argument with which to reach them. None.

My own thinking during these years was struggling with a double or triple problem. On the one hand I had found it necessary to face on an adult level some of the problems raised by the data of science. On the other hand I wished to be able to represent to men of science the reasons for belief. No such experience grows by careful logical steps — nor did mine. Rather, witness went along with struggle. Failure to be convincing in a particular discussion would sometimes force a change in outlook toward the function of an apologetics approach. Similarly, change in my view of the nature of science forced modification of claims in defense of belief.

For a time I planned on writing — and actually laid the foundations for — arguments in defense of belief in God. These arguments, I hoped, would be compelling. However, I gradually came to see both in epistemological theory and in practice that neither argument nor evidence (not even a resurrection from the dead) could prove God to one who chose not to believe, and I began to abandon that degree of reliance which I had previously placed on argumentation.

Instead I began to ask questions of the Scriptures: how can such men ever be convinced? Where are the effective weapons with which to reach them? The Scriptures clearly replied: not in philosophy, not in apologetics as such (useful though this is as supporting data), not in "words of man's wisdom" (I Corinthians 2:4).

Rather, the first chink in their armor lies elsewhere. There are certain kinds of truth which they find impossible to completely ignore, and which point in the direction of God: "By this shall all men *know* that ye are *my* disciples, if ye have love one to another" (John 13:35).

Christian kindness, gentleness, and thoughtfulness for others are a showcase of God's light which even an epistemology cannot completely screen off. "Ye are the light of the world" and "cannot be hid" (Matthew 5:14). "Ye are our epistles, known and read of all men" (II Corinthians 3:2). No wonder that God will go to extreme lengths to break us into that character mold! I began here to see *why* a "successful" Christian productive of energy and vigorous witness is just hot air (or, in Scriptural words, "sounding brass") unless his character is made up of the gentle fruits of the Spirit.

Nevertheless the verbal witness also is vital. Stout affirmation of belief in the content and factualness of the historical life, death, and actual bodily resurrection of Christ must form the heart of the message, which must be heard and accepted if one is to reach God. But this message must not be abused by being used as if it were an argument which is a "proof" in the logical sense. We have already seen that arguments cannot get deep enough under biases to be effective. How then does a witness ever succeed, if people are dead to it?

Here, it seems, a supernatural effort is necessary — a task beyond us. Only the Holy Spirit can move in a man's under-standing so that he sees truth in the story.

Do we have any clues as to the way He works to perform that task? I think so. In my own life the Holy Spirit has worked to develop an adult certainty of God precisely by insisting that I strive for gentleness. I know — by His inward working — that I have failed, but I know I am responsible. Something surely is needed for that, I sense. And when I read the Scriptures I find that some indefinable quality about them paints a picture of me which I recognize, and gives a remedy I need.

They force upon me not only the knowledge that I have sinned, but the inward conviction — worked in me by the Holy Spirit — of the truth of Christ's statement that He "came not to call the righteous but sinners to repentance" (Matthew 9:13). Nobody else but acknowledged sinners can hear Him.

All others are deaf. I am a sinner, and have heard, and I therefore believe in God who sent Christ to call to me.

But this certainly comes by faith through His working. By *faith*[2] — not by argument[3] — I know that the worlds are framed by the Word of God. By *faith* — not by apologetics — I know that these Scriptures are the Word of God. By *faith* — not by intellectual proof — I know that God, a Person who knows me by name, exists.

But how does this conviction work out in me? As nearly as I can tell — though I am aware that our understanding of ourselves is not to be fully trusted — I believe in God because the Holy Spirit has convicted me of sin, and has opened my eyes to see that the Scriptures truthfully point to Christ who came to take care of just that. Even so, Lord Jesus.

2. Faith cannot operate, however, without some component of intellectual appreciation of the truth of the historical events. My faith would not survive the complete intellectual destruction of my view of the historicity of the Scriptures. My faith would not survive if I were to believe — to use a crude example — that the Scriptures were written in 1250 A.D. Faith, however, cannot be replaced, as I see it, by intellectual "proof" — or the Scriptures themselves would thereby be discredited! This says nothing more, in principle, than a fact which we may be loath to accept — that "the natural man receiveth not the things of the Spirit of God: for they are foolishness unto him: neither can he know them, because they are spiritually discerned" (I Corinthians 2:14).

My own experience does no more than point up this Biblical principle (*cf.* also I Corinthians 1:21; 2:5) which has been known to other children of God through the centuries. This material is not intended to be "new" — it is new only in the sense that an automobile accident is "new" to a particular man the first time he is personally involved.

3. I have given up trying to reach the intellectuals by argument. Whenever I have tried to meet them on their own ground by beginning a discussion in which tentatively none of us assumed the existence of the personal nature of God and the validity of the Scriptures, I have failed to make much progress. It is difficult to bring such a line of argument to a point beyond a vague pantheistic "god," god as merely made up of the whole world of nature and of men, or even beyond the point where God is zero and we die like conditioned dogs. In order to come out with faith in God, the discussion must begin with God assumed. Then the line of argument may suggest an intellectual tidying up of some problems and implications of this view. I am convinced that by argument we cannot prove the existence of God to the unconvinced.

The attempt to maintain balance between trust in God as source of power and the responsibility of possessing vigor in one's daily work leads to personal struggle. Synthesis can be achieved only by recognizing the ultimate bankruptcy of one's own resources, along with trust in the fullness of God.

15 Earthen Vessels

APART FROM CHRIST, NOTHING OF ETERNAL VALUE CAN BE DONE by us or through us. As we think of work ahead of us, therefore, we need to realize our incompetence. Woe to us if we feel thoroughly competent to do God's job. We must realize that if anything is to be accomplished by us, it will be done only because God does it, for us, through us, and first of all *in* us. We are acceptable to serve God only when we know that we can do nothing.

This knowledge in itself has its dangers, because the moment that we say to ourselves, "I am nothing," we feel helpless as we realize that either we must change character, or be discarded like a broken vessel. After a vessel has baked, it can no longer be reworked, and broken pieces are tossed away. At this point, then, there is a danger that we will decide that we are like the broken pot already in the furnace, cooked, and without remedy. If we accept this of and by itself, we collapse in despair, quit, and in this way we are destroyed as productive members of the Christian community.

It is necessary, therefore, as in many other phases of the Christian life, that we keep before us a balance of two truths. On the one hand we must be torn to pieces until we realize that we are not competent. On the other hand we must realize that even though incompetent we must not quit, but look to Christ for encouragement, strength, and usefulness.

A verse which helps to encourage us in spite of our incompetence and hopelessness is Isaiah 42:3, "A bruised reed shall he not break, and the smoking flax shall he not quench."

The Lord takes this figure of the smoking flax as if, I think, He were in a little American Indian village, such as some which I have seen, where the people live in log cabins, or in still poorer shelters made with a thatch roof, four posts in the ground, and corn fodder leaning up against the eaves. That is all the protection there is against the cold mountain breeze.

In the middle of the night, if these people want to see (they cannot afford a candle — that would cost a penny; they cannot even afford a stick of special pitch-wood taken from the heart of a pine — that would cost part of a penny), they find three or four pieces of straw, and they put this straw against a live coal and blow on it until it breaks into flame. As it smokes and burns, a kind of light is made. But this burning straw is a painful kind of light. Its smoke hurts your eyes, and blackens the house. You may want to put it out, but if you do, you are left in the dark.

Christ sees us somewhat like this smoking flax, this burning straw, used as the poorest man's candle.

Who can be poorer than those who are in the darkness of a tribe without God's Word, with no one to tell them of Him? They are without light. Many people say, "Leave them alone; they are not worth the effort. They are too small. It is too expensive to reach them."

It is expensive. To reach them, people are needed who are strong, who have good personalities, and utmost capacity intellectually. They are needed to go out into the highways and byways and light candles for those in darkness. But people to be usable must first have learned a combination of capability and humility.

What does God do? He takes people who are of less quality, but broken, smoking flax. We are all smoking flax — or should be in our own eyes. God takes us and gives us a little light. So we have a little light, but along with it we have bad tempers, some of us; we have bad heart murmurs, some of us; we are nervous, we are too shy, or we are too bold. All of us make a lot of smoke, but in spite of that God has chosen us. Now what is He going to do with us?

The logical thing to do would be to put us out — to quench

the smoking flax. But this He does not do. He takes us and
sends us to a little cabin where a poor man lives who has no
candle. And He uses us. Our Lord does not quench the
smoking flax.

Some of us are like a stick that a hiker is using as a cane.
When a hiker comes to a hole, he uses a stick to let a foot
down easily. If the stick is poor, it collapses, and the hiker
cannot lean on it. But if we are like such a stick, God does
not throw us away. He has not come to destroy us but to
salvage us. "A bruised reed shall he not break" (Isaiah 42:3).

We are told this, in different terms, in many parts of the
Scripture. "Therefore seeing we have this ministry, as we have
received mercy, we faint not" (II Corinthians 4:1). And, "But
we have this treasure in earthen vessels, that the excellency of
the power may be of God, and not of us" (4:7).

If we were golden vessels, boasting with self-wisdom, self-
justification, ability and competence, we would not be able to
hold this power, because His power cannot be held in a proud
vessel. "But God hath chosen the foolish things of the world
to confound the wise; and God hath chosen the weak things
of the world to confound the things which are mighty; and
the base things of the world, and things which are despised, hath
God chosen, yea, and things which are not, to bring to nought
things that are: that no flesh should glory in his presence. But
of him are ye in Christ Jesus, who of God is made unto us
wisdom, and righteousness, and sanctification, and redemption"
(I Corinthians 1:27-30).

Being emptied, earthen vessels, recognizing our limitations,
we can get power from God. That is to say, He chose us
because we are weak, *not in spite of* the fact. He chose us
because we are weak, since if we see that we are weak, we are
able to seek for His power until we are strong (II Corinthians
4:16-18, and 12:5-10).

As you go to bed tonight, if suddenly you are struck with
the thought that you are unable to do the task, you may start
to say, "Lord, thank you for choosing me in spite of my miserable self." Change that prayer on occasion (that prayer is
all right, too, sometimes), to say, "Lord, thank you for choosing me because I am weak, so that You can show your power
and not get it mixed up with mine."

With energy directed towards service to God, even failure may not represent destruction. Outward failure may be a manifested variant of inward success. Courage to continue comes from deeper sources than outward results.

16 When Failure Is Success

IN LANGUAGES THERE ARE HOMONYMS — WORDS WHICH SOUND alike but mean something quite different. In behavior, also actions which look alike may be of different character in relation to the world and to God.

The Scriptures clearly show us that there are such homonym-like actions which are relevant to the Christian. The portion defining this with which we are most familiar is I Corinthians 13: "Though I speak with the tongues of men and of angels, and have not charity, I am become as sounding brass, or a tinkling cymbal."

Within our activity we may have the bearing of a religious person, we may speak the words of a religious person, but if within our hearts we are not interested in others, then we are not living according to the will of God.

The life of one person may be "homophonous" with that of somebody else. He may look just as religious, he may do the same things, he may say the same words; and yet the first person may be pleasing to God and the other be rejected by God. The difference has to do with the purpose of his actions, the intent of his heart.

An action plus its purpose makes up a unit. God is interested in the total unit and its impact on society. Just as we are interested in the meaning without which homophonous words are "the same," so God is interested in the intent without which some activities are "the same."

Two activities identical in outward view may be extremely different one from another. For example, a filibuster in the

Senate may sound the same as an ordinary speech, but the purpose is different. So it may be with persons. In I Samuel 16:7 Samuel was looking on the outward appearance of the older sons of Jesse, and to him they all looked like possible kings. But God was looking on their hearts, and there was something different in David's heart, something about the purposes behind his actions, that made it possible for him to please God.

Now the opposite point is this: a word — or the meaningful part of a word — may be found in two variants which sound quite different but mean the same. In linguistics we call the variants "allomorphs." There is an "s" on *cups*, an "en" on *oxen* and an "es" on *houses*, and they are "the same," the plural marker of the word, even though they are pronounced and spelled differently. What ties them together? The fact that they all designate the plural and function in the same suffix slot. It is this meaning and function that identify them as the same.

In other kinds of behavior also it is the intent and function which make different actions to be recognized as structurally the same. Two actions might not be recognized as the same basic unit, functionally, because the outward appearances are different, or because the times of the action are different. The Lord had to tell His disciples to be careful about this. When some persons were preaching in the name of Christ but not following the disciples in their particular attitude or method, the disciples were ready to stop them because these people were different and therefore seemed "wrong." But the Lord Jesus warned the disciples that even though these people were different they could be one with the disciples — "allomorphs" of the Body of Christ, variant manifestations of His church and likewise doing His work.

We have to be careful, therefore, when we try to identify a person for what he is. *We* cannot see intent. But God deals with the heart, and in differentiating one person's contribution from that of another He includes their intent and purpose.

Have you ever felt defeat? You will some day — the world is too big to live long without sensing failure. In the face of enormous work to be done, some of us will fail. Some of us accomplish "nothing." There is no cause to worry, if the intent of the heart and the thrust of the will are to serve God.

If our trust is in God and our activity is aimed at serving God, and not at serving our self-esteem — then if there is "failure" it is actually a variety of "success." In God's sight *this* kind of defeat, when beyond our control, may prove to be an "allomorph" of the very success we seek. The "last" may here be "first."

God looks on the heart, and that is to our benefit when our hearts are right but is not to our benefit if we are trying to get by on a pious exterior. It is not to our benefit if our righteousness is made up of form — of counting the hours of service instead of serving because people need our help. The scribes and Pharisees had the form, the outward trappings, but the intent of the heart was lacking.

Let us be careful. Mere form of activity will not prove that we are righteous; it has to be the heart. Let us be considerate of Christian brethren. Even though they "follow not us," their intent may be the same.

How strange that hope — one of the big three of I Corinthians 13:13 — should be so little talked about! Yet here lies power for patience.

17 Hope

"Now abideth faith, hope, love, these three; but the greatest of these is love" (I Corinthians 13:13). Faith is important (Hebrews 11), but what about hope? Why is it listed among the big three?

We stand on faith in order to build a present edifice of hope. Faith is not the building.

Before the Sadducees and Pharisees, Paul said, "I am a Pharisee, the son of a Pharisee: of the hope and resurrection of the dead I am called in question" (Acts 23:6). Later he said, "I stand and am judged for the hope. . ." (Acts 26:6). Paul was judged for *hope*, not just for faith. It is not just the faith of our fathers for which we die — it is the hope!

Perhaps the reason why some people with apparent faith are so glum is that they have forgotten about hope. They have thrown away thirty percent of their heritage. They have kept their faith. They have tried to be gentle, and decent, and have love, but they have neglected hope as one point of focus. This they should not do. Rejoice in hope!

Without hope a person can trust and still be glum. He can say, "God has told me to do this," and he does it because he is supposed to. He can leave Sodom and head for the mountains at the command of God — and look back, glum. That is dangerous. Hope looks to the hills — to the harvest. "He that ploweth should plow in hope" (I Corinthians 9:10).

Hope does not start in full flower, however. There must be growth. The start is likely to be with faith, in trial. Then, if in difficulties we stand firm (knowing that God is in control regardless of who the earthly dictator or boss seems to be) we receive patience. (Not "patience" in the sense of not getting angry, but patience in the sense of steadfastness in the face of

problems, difficulties, trials.)   By continuously standing firm
we gain experience.   From this experience we gradually learn
that things not only work out all right in the sense that we
will somehow get through life in spite of evil.   But what is
more, we learn that they work out all right in the sense that
God has deliberately allowed evil in the world to stimulate us
to do what we would not otherwise do, and to discover what
we would not otherwise discover.

When I try to think of what we would be like if we had
no evil around us, the best I can do is to imagine that we would
all be holy — which we are not now.   In addition we would —
perhaps — be sitting on a mountain top, playing a flute and
watching the sheep graze.   Nothing more.   But God does not
allow us to be like that.   He needles us with evil, stimulates
us to work, drives us to compete, shames us when people without God's power available to them go beyond us.

So we get experience, and this experience enables us to see
that, in the long run, God takes us through.   Once we have
really learned this, *this* is hope.   Thus we see the growth:
"Tribulation worketh patience; patience, experience; and experience hope" (Romans 5:4).

Only the conviction that self is not lost before God in some deep nirvana, but is ever vibrantly particular, individual, permanent — only such a conviction that God knows us and appreciates us by name will eventually allow hope to remain and the commitment for service before Him to be most deeply rewarded.

18 The Individual

ONE DAY I SAID THAT EVERY PART OF THE BIBLE HAD A MESSAGE for us — all of it was profitable.

A friend asked, "What do you get out of the genealogies?"

"A great thrill," I replied. And this is it. . . .

When we talk about the Bible, the people we mention most are those like Moses, Abraham, Daniel, and Paul. Few of us are great enough to fit into the category with them, and sometimes we are prone to ask ourselves, "What about me? Do I count? Do I really matter to God?"

Yes. The genealogies give evidence that we do. The first nine chapters of I Chronicles contain lists of people who were not great but who counted. For the most part only names and relationships are given: "And the sons of Helah were Zereth, Izhar, and Ethnan" (I Chronicles 4:7, ARV). But in the midst of the genealogy an occasional incident is recorded, "And Jabez called on the God of Israel, saying, Oh that thou wouldest bless me indeed . . . and that thou wouldest keep me from evil . . . and God granted him that which he requested" (I Chronicles 4:10, ARV). God did so, even though Jabez was like us — just an ordinary person.

I Chronicles 11:20-22 (ARV) has another list of names and accounts of people: "And Abishai . . . lifted up his spear against three hundred and slew them . . . Benaiah the son of Jehoiada, the son of a valiant man of Kabzeel, who had done mighty deeds, he slew the two sons of Ariel of Moab." These men had courage and God helped them, and their names went down in the record forever.

Then there was the woman who poured the precious ointment on Jesus' head (Matthew 26:7-13, ARV). And some of the disciples objected, asking, "To what purpose is this waste?" And Jesus said, "She hath wrought a good work upon me . . . Wheresoever this gospel shall be preached in the whole world, that also which this woman hath done shall be spoken of for a memorial of her." And her sacrifice has not been forgotten.

Sacrifices which we make as we try to serve the Lord are not wasted. They are recorded — like this: "Jashobeam the son of a Hachmonite, the chief of the thirty; he lifted up his spear against three hundred and slew them one at a time" (I Chronicles 11:11, ARV).

Little-known folk are known in heaven; they are not lost. They are remembered there; they are not thrown into a sea of people whose faces merge into a mass. In heaven it does not say, "In the year 1962 a large number of people were serving the Lord as members of a certain denomination." Not at all! We are known by name. God looks at us and He says, "There is John, and George, and Ted, and Susie."

Where does the Bible tell us that God does that? Let me read it to you: "Adam, Seth, Enosh, Kenan, Mahalalel, Jared, Enoch, Methuselah, Lamech, Noah, Shem, Ham, and Japheth" (I Chronicles 1:1, 2).

Other religions are not like that. In Buddhism a person is like a drop of water taken temporarily out of the ocean. In trouble on earth he longs for the day when that drop will fall back into the ocean. There it will dissipate, its molecules will disappear, and the personality represented by that drop will be gone.

With Christianity that is not so. Heaven is not like that. In heaven we are still people. How do I know? I know from the Word of God. "Shammoth the Harorite, Helez the Pelonite, Ira the son of Ikkesh the Tekote, Abiezer the Anathothite, Sibbecai . . ." (I Chronicles 11:27, 28, ARV).

Whoever heard of Sibbecai? God has heard of him, and He has written his name in a Book of remembrance. In that

Book you can find a list of those who gave to the tabernacle, and what they gave (Numbers 7). You can find a list of those who went back to the promised land (Ezra 2). You can find a list of those who took up their places to repair the wall of Jerusalem (Nehemiah 3). You do not remember their names. Of course you do not — you are just a man. But God remembers.

He has promised to remember. In Isaiah 49:14-16 (ARV) Zion said, "The Lord hath forgotten me." But the answer comes back, "Can a woman forget her sucking child? . . . Yea, these may forget, yet will not I forget thee. Behold, I have graven thee upon the palms of my hands." Your name is there, right where He can look at it. He will not forget.

I can forget. I even mix up the names of my own children. It makes them so annoyed when I call Barbara "Judith," and Judith "Barbara."

When my mother was trying to get the attention of one of her children, I heard her say, on occasion, "Otto, Galen, Reginald, Ezra — Kenneth, stop that!" My mother occasionally mixed up the eight of us, but God does not even mix up two billion of us.

"What doest thou here, Elijah?" He gently asked that frightened man (I Kings 19:9, ARV). And to you He says, "What are you doing here, Joe? And you, Bill? And you, Ruth?" And He gets your name right every time!

God is not going to forget. Hebrews 6:10 (Montgomery) tells us that He will not. "For God is not unjust; he will not forget your work and the love you showed for his cause, in sending help to your fellow Christians, as you are still doing."

He will not forget those who are to enter the New Jerusalem. "There will not enter it anything profane, nor any who work abominations and a lie; but only those who are written in the Lamb's Book of Life" (Revelation 21:27, Montgomery). Did you notice? Only those shall enter whose *names* have been recorded. Yours and mine are there. We are listed, individually.

God has let us see some of His lists: "And Abraham begat Isaac. The sons of Isaac; Esau, and Israel. The sons of Esau; Eliphaz, Reuel, and Jeush, and Jalam, and Korah. The sons of Eliphaz: Teman, and Omar, Zephi, and Gatam, Kenaz, and

Timna, and Amalek" (I Chronicles 1:34-36, ARV). Time fails me to read more of these, but join with me in praising God for His interest in us, and that we live as individuals before Him.

PART IV: OUTREACH

*Integration with God and man de-
mands service to others. Yet inborn
resistance to outward service makes
all such tasks a struggle. We must
try to improve the circumstances of
our neighbor — at our expense if
necessary — rather than try to obtain
status at the cost of his happiness.*

19 Serving Our Colleagues

ZACCHAEUS WAS SERVING HIMSELF IN THE BEGINNING OF THE STORY
in Luke 19, but then the Holy Spirit worked in his heart.
And we find that his personality was different after the Holy
Spirit had worked in him for a while. In the end, as far as
this story goes, Zacchaeus was serving others. Not only was
he replacing that which he had stolen, but he was serving beyond the line of duty.

Then there was Nicodemus. He had to be born again (John
3), have his whole outlook changed, and start all over with
Jesus. Without trying to understand all this, he spread his
sails to the power. And in John 19 we find Nicodemus serving, bringing spices for Jesus' body — not a prominent task for
an intellectual, but the "greatest among you shall be your
servant" (Matthew 23:11).

Using our twentieth-century language, we can say that one
means of serving our colleagues is to make them "look good"
in the eyes of others at our own expense.

I have a young boy, and every once in a while he wants to
climb up on my shoulders. When he is up there, he may shout
with delight: "Mommy, Mommy, look at me. I am taller than
Daddy!" On my shoulders he has a foundation from which
he stands head and shoulders above anybody else, including
me. He has been made to look good. He has been made to
look tall and mature. And suddenly, by climbing on someone
else's shoulders, he feels, in a small way, part of the adult community.

Pride often tempts us to make ourselves appear good in the eyes of the public at the expense of our colleagues. In fact, we may not only try to make ourselves appear good, but we may even make one of our colleagues look "sick" that we might appear better. This is not the will of God; rather the will of God for us is to serve — to make others, not ourselves, look good. The will of God is not that we look good, or important, or successful. Rather, the will of God is that we make ourselves shoulders on which our colleagues can climb so that they look good, and powerful, and successful, and productive.

None of us lives in a vacuum, none of us lives to himself and none of us exists on his own. The great sin of Adam and Eve was to want to be independently good in their own eyes. That same sin plagues us, but we cannot be independently good. None of us can hope to be head and shoulders above anybody else except as we are standing on the shoulders of someone who is our foundation. Not only is the Lord our foundation, but our colleagues are also.

Only a few can be the shoulders for all. There are only a few to whom God has given the grace to stand when everybody discourages them. But all of us with encouragement from one another can in turn give encouragement to others. We can encourage the others and help them to look good, not that they might be proud, but that they might produce for the glory of God.

It is amazing how a little courage helps us produce. Only a few go ahead without encouragement. The rest of us need it, for it is the encouragement from others that gives the courage without which most of us are not men, and without which we collapse in the face of trouble. Most people are not independent enough to stand without such help. Hence others need to uphold them, to let them climb on their shoulders until they can get up above the crowd, until they can see what it is like to be as tall as somebody else. They need a genuine compliment, a genuine bit of appreciation, genuine encouragement. It is amazing how we want to have esteem in the eyes of our colleagues.

When I was a freshman in college, I was part of a crew that served tables in the cafeteria, and a couple of the crew were the most accomplished fellows at barbed comments that I have ever met.

In competition with them I became clever, too, and by the end of that year I could not hear a sentence from one of my colleagues without thinking of something clever and sharp with which to reply. When my Dad heard me, he would say, "Why do people not study to say the kind thing instead of the cruel thing?" But I could not think of anything encouraging, or sweet, or good. I had become totally corrupt. I could think only of the cruel thing, the clever thing, at which people had to laugh even if they were hurt.

I saw after a while that I was losing all my friends, and I asked God to break me of that habit. It took three years to break it, and in order to do so I had to swear before God that I would be silent rather than say something barbed and cruel. I was not used to being silent and it hurt to have nothing to say when I was bursting with a clever remark. But God does not want us to look clever at the expense of someone else. We are called to serve, to make others look good.

All of salvation is to make us look good! We who are dirty, worn, broken, and sinful are to be the showcase of heaven. The angels are watching to see God take somebody who is not good and make him look good. "Who art thou that judgest another man's servant? . . . He shall be holden up: for God is able to make him stand" (Romans 14:4).

The Lord Jesus came to serve. As the chief, He was the slave; as above all, He was the door-mat. And He said an amazing thing to His followers, "Greater things than these shall ye do."

His are the shoulders on which we stand, and when He said, "Greater things than these shall ye do," He meant it. Did He ever get outside His home country and go beyond? No. When were the big crowds won and redeemed by His blood? At Pentecost, after He had gone. Did He ever translate the Bible for anybody? No.

Today we are bringing the Word of God to tribes that have never had it. And why shouldn't we, with His shoulders to stand on, and with His power to work from? He did not have His own resurrection behind Him. His blood redemption which is behind us was not there until He was through. He learned obedience in order to be a foundation stone for us, and that we might go beyond. He was a slave; He came to die that we might live.

What does Matthew 10:39 mean? "He that findeth his life shall lose it," and Matthew 19:30, "But many that are first shall be last; and the last shall be first." He who looks good is going to look bad, if he has been standing on other people when he should have been under them supporting them.

Some of us feel that we are not very important. We do not get good grades. We have not led a lot of people to the Lord. We are not powerful speakers. We are not in the public eye. We do not seem to look good.

In this there is no need to fear. The ones who are going to look good in heaven are not necessarily the ones who look good here.

The ones who are going to look good in heaven are the ones who have won the inward battle. They are the ones who have a life full of love, and make others look good instead of themselves. They are the ones who are full of joy, instead of grouching; full of gentleness, rather than toughness. They are the ones who have self-control; studying when they should study; going to bed when they should go to bed; getting up when they should get up; reading the Bible when they should read the Bible. They make their bodies mind them.

When on the field, these people, under self-control, throw down their books to be with the people who need their attention. They do not say, "I have got to study, I cannot talk with you." And yet when the people are gone and time is available, then they sit down, open their books, dig in and translate. They study and learn verbs when their time is their own, instead of taking two hours out for a cup of coffee.

These are they who shall be first in heaven. Not those who are clever, not those who look good on earth.

And on the field are new Christians. Do we make them look good and feel good?

I cannot erase from my memory the dull anger and hurt I felt once. I was on the shores of a lake in Latin America. I was with a missionary whom I knew only slightly, when a boy about ten years old came up to me with a little boat made out of reeds. It was a lovely little boat with a mast made out of a stick. He held it up to me in a genuine, friendly way and asked, "You want to buy my boat?"

And I did want to buy his boat; it was pretty and he had made it. I could have had it for almost nothing, although the money I paid would have been a good bit to the boy. But as I started to buy it, the missionary grabbed it. He snatched it without permission! He pulled off the mast and said, "That is not worth the money, it is no good!" And he gave it back to the boy.

That missionary had just been released from jail. He had been put there, supposedly, for teaching the name of the Lord. But no wonder he had been in jail! He had not learned that we should not make the harmless customs of the nationals of other countries appear ugly at points where they are merely different from our own. He needed to learn gentleness, surrender, consideration of others; he needed to learn to encourage what is good, and pure, and lovely. He needed to learn that we should be patient while the Lord is working in others, just as He must in us, to eliminate that which is dark. All of us must somehow learn His lessons.

The Lord chose His twelve, most of them just ordinary men. He sent them forth and said, "Greater things than these shall ye do," and He let them stand on His shoulders. And in our relationships with believers, we must let those who will become leaders stand on our shoulders, rather than keeping ourselves head and shoulders over them. Then greater things than we they shall do.

*Natural man seeks a top place in
power. Christian man is commanded
to be a servant. This change makes
last first, first last, and turns criteria
of society structure upside down.
Selfishness gives way to the outreach
of directed love.*

20   Turning Society Upside Down

EVEN THE BARNYARD DEVELOPS A "SOCIETY." ONE CHICKEN PECKS
another — and it pecks back; and another pecks that one and it
pecks back. Presently one pecks so hard that, instead of peck-
ing back, the weaker one runs and pecks a chick that may be
less in size or power. The lesser one may peck back once or
twice, but then it, too, waits for a chick still smaller. At the
bottom there may be a chicken, weak and sad, who runs to
hide under the coop because there is nobody it can peck safely.
This type of structure in fowl society is known as "The Peck
Order."[1]

I was astonished some time ago when I read a theoretical book
by Nadel on the theory of social structure.[2] He was trying
to develop a theory which would allow him to analyze all of
society in some one simple way. He talked about role
analysis, about the various parts that people play in society.
He wanted to abstract from the material the simplest component which would be relevant, not just to the characterization
of one particular society, but to all kinds of society.

When he had accomplished his progressive layers of abstrac-
tion he reached a diagnostic component of roles in reference to
"mere command differentials."[3] He says, "And if, in view of
this, it is argued that the 'social structure' I am envisaging is
little more than a power, authority or status structure, I would

1. See "The Social Order of Chickens," *Scientific American,* 194:2:43-46
(1956).
2. *The Theory of Social Structure* (Glencoe, Ill., 1957), pp. 115-24.
3. *Ibid.,* p. 124.

reply that this seems to me the only 'dimension' both sufficiently abstract for our purpose and still sufficiently relevant, in the sense of being important in human and social existence."[4] Now, he was not interested in saying anything specific, as I am doing, about "motivations or desires inherent in human nature." He was making "no assumptions whatever about people's love of command or thirst for power."[5] This was not his task. He was just trying to describe what he saw, and the only universal component that he could find that would describe the heart of human society structure was command differential which I may summarize as: I boss you, you boss somebody else; I give deference and benefits to you, you give deference to somebody else. This seems to me to imply the presence of a human variety of a Peck Order.

In the Scriptures an observation related to Nadel's is worth noting: the mother of the sons of Zebedee came to Jesus and asked that they be allowed to be on His right hand and on His left (Matthew 20:20-25), and "there was also a strife among [the disciples], which of them should be accounted the greatest" (Luke 22:24). They were becoming deeply involved in the human power struggle. Jesus explained the problem to them somewhat like this, "You do not know what you are asking for. The power structure of which I am a part is not the kind of thing you think it is; it includes difficulty." And, "Ye know that the princes of the Gentiles exercise dominion over them, and they that are great exercise authority upon them." Principles for a Christian society must be set up on the following terms, "Whosoever will be great among you, let him be your minister; and whosoever will be chief among you, let him be your servant: even as the Son of man came not to be ministered unto, but to minister, and to give his life a ransom for many" (Matthew 20:25-28).

In the non-Christian order, furthermore, "they that exercise authority upon them are called benefactors" (Luke 22:25). I was given in Ciudad Trujillo, a few years ago, a pamphlet for tourists which called Trujillo "benefactor." Why, if such a ruler was in fact a tyrant? Even the tyrant recognizes

4. *Ibid.*, pp. 121-22.
5. *Ibid.*, p. 122.

that true lordship *ought* to flow from service. He tries hypo-critically to pose as if he were at the top of that service order rather than at the top of sheer brute power.

Man knows that it is wrong when a tyrant calls himself a benefactor. Man also knows that it is wrong when a Christian tries to lord it over the flock. Is part of the reason that, as a church, we are being driven out of parts of Asia, or maybe Africa, due to the fact that we never learned this lesson well enough? Patronizing attitudes make people furious; they know that Christians should not act that way. They know instinc-tively that the *good* man should be at the bottom of the Peck Order, not at the top.

So we see a "Peck Order" in the society of man, but we see a different order in the society of the kingdom of heaven. The order into which we were born as fallen man is to be turned upside down in the order of God. "Many that are first shall be last, and the last shall be first" (Matthew 19:30). He who has chosen for rewards a status at the top of the Peck Order will be at the bottom of the Christian order. "Verily I say unto you, They have their reward" (Matthew 6:5).

God Himself follows the principle that He inculcates in us. He is not grabby for power. In Philippians we are told that God would not take the right to be at the top of the power hierarchy, and Jesus Christ, as God, took the bottom place in that hierarchy — He emptied himself of power-rights and took a servant's place (2:6-7). He chose not to come to earth as a king — because from our point of view He might then have appeared to be thirsting for place at the top of the power hierarchy. He had to come as a servant, without money, with-out bed, without friends, so that even in our eyes He would be at the bottom in status, but top in service.

"Let this mind be in you, which was also in Christ Jesus" (Philippians 2:5).

In the process of serving others we find that we become part of a team. By ourselves very little of importance can be accomplished. Yet we find that integration with the abilities and tasks of our neighbors in life's game requires delicate adjustments of personal esteem and acceptance of place. Such a team finds God involved as one of the players — senior to us, but leaving us with a substantial role to fill.

21 Players

"WE ARE GOD'S FELLOW WORKERS" (I CORINTHIANS 3:9). WITH Him we work to achieve His purpose. With Him, it would seem, we should never fail. And yet we do, and this failure makes us want to understand more about a plan of God which can even include failure.

The Scriptures draw on the sports world for a number of helpful illustrations: wrestling (Ephesians 6:12), foot racing (Philippians 3:14; I Corinthians 9:24 ff.), boxing (I Corinthians 9:26), the athlete's crown (II Timothy 4:8; I Peter 5:4; Revelation 2:10).

Modern sports may help us with further figures of speech about teamwork — since, as fellow workers with God, we may assume that we are on His "team." That is, we are part of a team on which God is the Senior Player. He is the most experienced, the most powerful, the most capable. He is its Captain.

Seldom are all players on a volleyball team equally good. Some are strong and some are weak; some are tall "spikers" and some short retrievers. Yet when the team wins, the weakest player wins just as truly as the strongest. He gets a share of the credit, and his name is inscribed on the cup.

I am on the team, but it is not a question of whether God wins or loses. The question is, will the team win or lose? We are teammates with God. If the team wins, I win, even though I have made blunders. The team is going to win because God is on it. Just as surely as He is the Captain, the team has the balance of power for obtaining the title.

And yet a particular game can be lost (and sometimes is) if a weaker player, feeling that his contribution does not amount to enough to be worth his total effort, fails to work hard enough.

The Captain must be able to count on each person's contribution and be able to assign special responsibilities in the heat of the game: "Watch the net! Careful, leave the center to me, but cover that far corner as best you can." Vital roles remain for the weak, roles which may include playing in spots where they occasionally muff the ball if it comes hard their way. If one should fail to try, sulking because of the more glorious successes of teammates, he may be benched. The Captain chose him with total team stamina over a long period of time in mind. And the Captain senses the moment when a brief replacement or support of strong by weak can allow the strong later to score in full power, or when the weak may partially cover the empty corners.

But why does our Captain let us, the weak, fail? Does He not have power to protect us against every attack, to handle every difficult ball which comes our way? Did He not say to Pilate, "You would have no power over me unless it had been given you from above" (John 19:11)? And is it not true that nobody can take the ball away from us, unless our Captain lets him? Why then does He?

Part of the answer seems to be that without such exercise we would be weak. We grow strong by struggling against obstacles and difficult odds.

But a more subtle part of the answer, perhaps a less important part, however, may be seen in the human reaction that if all the good players are on one side, it is no fun. Players in a game want to participate in a close game. They may want to win, but they also want worthy competition. The game becomes boring if there is no struggle. Nor do they want any one player to handle the ball all the time, every game, and make all the plays by himself (even if he could). Each player wants to play his part in a vigorous battle. The Christian life, it seems to me, has been designed with this trait of man in mind. We are in a game which is grim, a battle in which it is terribly important whether we win or lose. Just so, if our Captain were to handle the ball every time, and inevitably made a point, and if He always returned every difficult ball of the opposition, nobody would get excited. There would be no competition. There would in fact, from the human viewpoint, be no point in scheduling the game at all. We would not have any "breathless interest" in the Christian life if everything were won before we started. We would say, "What are we playing for? The ball never gets to us — He takes it all the time!" So He stands aside much of the time. He lets the opposing team do well, so that we as His teammates can fight the battle, a battle with clash and risk of broken bones.

Of course, we may miss a play or get hurt, and others get hurt because of us, but still we want to try. The Christian life might pall if there were no battle, not because we wickedly desire excitement, but because God has created us to be alive, to be vigorous participants in life, to climb a steep, narrow, rocky trail rather than roll down an easy incline like an inanimate stone loosened by the frost. This interest in the difficult game, when the desire is under His control, is a gift from Him.

We sometimes fail to realize when it is our play. We do not always take the opportunities that we have been given. For example, the men in the Garden of Gethsemane were on a "team" with Jesus, and He was having a hard time, and He wanted their help (Matthew 26:37, 38). A time comes when even a strong player needs somebody to cover a corner. The game was hard even for Him. But instead of fighting the battle with Him, His teammates fell asleep.

Of course, it was easy for them to sleep, since it was the custom in their culture to sleep on the ground. And it is easy for us to fall asleep instead of fighting the battle. We are in bed, too, in our culture. Western culture is our bed of ease, and in it we sleep instead of taking the initiative in the struggle. As members of the team it is up to us to work and to do what we can while we have opportunity. We "must work the works of him who sent me, while it is day; night comes, when no one can work" (John 9:4). As long as we have light, we work. As long as we have health, we work. As long as we have an open door, we enter. As long as we have work to do, we do it, happy to be on the team.

We see that our Captain is aware of our individual problems. "When Jesus saw her weeping, and the Jews who came with her also weeping, he was deeply moved in spirit and troubled" (John 11:33). God responds to trouble on the local scene. In spite of having to uphold all the universe, He looks at one little local spot and He weeps.

We need His sympathetic help as we work, for sometimes we do not understand the game very well. Above all, we do not understand the Captain's strategy. What is going on? What is happening, anyhow? We do not understand, but we will later on: "For our knowledge is imperfect and our prophecy is imperfect . . . For now we see in a mirror dimly, but then face to face. Now I know in part; then I shall understand fully, even as I have been fully understood" (I Corinthians 13:9, 12, RSV).

Individual players on a team cannot see the whole playing area. Nor can we see the over-all strategy of our Captain in a struggle which embraces the universe for its playing field, and millennia for the periods of play.

Meanwhile, we must play our part until the going is too hard for us. Then the Captain may come our way with force to help meet the opposition. See? He will not let the other team win. They will not win, not because of the team, but because of our Captain: "All authority in heaven and on earth has been given to me. Go therefore" — and play the game.

There is no need to worry about the outcome. Play hard. He is on our side for the ultimate task entrusted to the team: teaching "all nations" to observe all that the Captain of our salvation has commanded.

When trying to carry out our part in the game, we find some of our tasks and outlooks difficult to reconcile. Drives from intellect and from devotion may clash. Walking does not lead to cold neutralization of energy, but to an oscillation from one point of rest to another. So the intellectual-devotional synthesis requires vigorous energy extended in both directions, each at its proper moment.

22 Walking

WALKING IS AN INTERESTING PROCEDURE. IT IS A RAPID VIBRATION between points of weight placement, such that the result gives us an even course. It is smooth. We put all our weight on one foot, then all our weight on the other foot, shifting so rapidly that it does not seem to be a vibration.

We do not walk — normally — on just one foot. It would be awkward to go very far that way. A useful walk does not favor one foot, nor do we tie our two feet together in order to walk. We do not normally try to walk carrying all our weight on both feet at the same time — if we did, we could not move. But neither is walking hitting a "happy medium." Happy medium has no place in a walk.

I am astonished when I study the life of Christ to see how He did not "strike a happy medium." It seems to me He was "all out" in every direction at once. He could be vigorous in condemnation of wrong while He was dreadfully sorry about what would happen to the wrongdoer. He could work from morning until night, and yet take time off to pray. Whatever His hand found to do, He did it with His might. He had balance. He got it by doing everything intensely, and the very intensities balanced each other. He was all man, and He was all God. All in all. All in total balance.

Those of us in school should be in balance, all out scholasti-
cally, but all out spiritually, too. If our total weight is always
on our academic foot, we will be cold and ultimately we will
be lonely. But the Christian walk is not just a spiritual walk.
That, too, would be hopping on one foot. The person who
tries to be just spiritual without the balancing characteristics
of human life becomes a crackpot. It is dangerous to lack balance. One needs to be a Christian so that his basic premises —
the beginning of wisdom — might rest on God, and be geared
into God's power. But one also needs continually to study the
Word vigorously, as a scholar worshipping the Lord with his
mind. He should be vigorous in devotion — with complete
trust in God. He should be vigorous in scholarship — using
his mind. He should be vigorous in friendship — including being friendly to those who are unfriendly to him.

The book of Ephesians starts out by telling us that we are
redeemed, that we have been made clean, that we have become
God's children, that we are geared into the universe. Then,
after these things, it says, "For we are his workmanship, created
in Christ Jesus unto good works, which God hath before or-
dained that we should *walk in them*" (Ephesians 2:10).

Thus in the first chapter we are told of the things which God
has done for us. Later we find that the balance of this truth
is that we ourselves are expected to do good things. Just as
God has helped us, we are expected to help others. That
makes the balance which is a part of walking. "I therefore,
the prisoner of the Lord, beseech you that ye *walk worthy* of
the vocation wherewith ye are called" (Ephesians 4:1). The
manner of walking is defined for us as with "lowliness and meek-
ness" (not being proud or jealous when someone gets ahead of
us), "with long suffering" (not getting upset when somebody
is irritating), "forbearing one another in love" (when they are
hard to live with). Having "unity" with those not of like
mind, instead of getting annoyed with them. We need to be
friends of people, so that we can serve them as we are ordered
to do.

"This I say therefore, and testify in the Lord, that ye hence-
forth walk not as other Gentiles walk . . ." (Ephesians 4:17).
The old life has been dirty; the new walk must be clean. The
old walk has been proud; the new walk must be humble. The

old walk has been for self; the new walk is for God and for other people. "And walk in love, as Christ also hath loved us, and hath given himself for us an offering and a sacrifice to God for a sweetsmelling savour" (Ephesians 5:2). So this walk, we are told, is to be a sacrificial walk, a walk of love. Then almost immediately the emphasis shifts firmly. Verse 6 says, "Let no man deceive you with vain words." We are not to be gullible and easily fooled. We are to be in balance, both "wise as serpents, and harmless as doves" (Matthew 10: 16). We are to be eager to do good and help others, but wise enough to avoid traps that have been laid for us. Christ sidestepped the traps which were laid for Him by the Pharisees ("This they said . . . that they might have to accuse him," John 8:6; "Is it lawful to give tribute unto Caesar, or not?" Matthew 22:17). But at the same time He fulfilled the law (Matthew 17:25-27). He was balanced in His walk. In Ephesians 5:8 we are told to walk as children of light, with goodness and truth and separation from evil. Yet in verses 15-17 we are told to "walk circumspectly, not as fools, but as wise . . . understanding what the will of the Lord is."

Christ in His walk did not strike a "happy medium." Rather, He was intense in every area of His life — in His reliance on the Father's orders, in using His own voice of authority, in His service to man, in His love for others, in his down-to-earth practical wisdom. Peter tells us that Christ is our example and that we should follow in His steps, walking as He walked (I Peter 2:21).

Each individual must seek for himself his own avenue of outreach. For me, an interest in language led by devious paths to the attempt to translate the Scriptures for small tribal groups in hidden corners of the world, where the people had no alphabet, primer, textbooks, or even — sometimes — interpreters. The Wycliffe Bible Translators, with whom I am associated in this phase of my interests, are currently working in about 250 languages, and hoping to work in 2,000. In any such endeavor practical questions arise. One of them here concerns the justification of the energy spent in long years of translation. Why not use English instead? The answer to those who know the international situation is obvious on political grounds. On cultural grounds there are equally important answers. Only through his mother tongue does a person respond quickly and deeply to the most crucial parts of life. Whereas in the laboratory one finds access to the structure of sticks, frogs, and atoms, through the mother tongue one finds access to values of love, joy, peace, hope, and the power of God.

23 We Will Tell Them, But in What Language?

PEOPLE WHO HAVE NEVER BEEN TO THE MISSION FIELD OFTEN ASK, *Why do you not teach the native peoples English instead of taking so much time to learn their language?*

Such a question is a legitimate one — especially if only a small number of people speak the language in question — and it deserves an answer.

It is usually not wise, for political reasons, to introduce large-scale teaching of English to aboriginal groups, because it hinders the governments' attempts to teach the people the national language or the trade language. It has also aroused suspicion of spying or imperialistic attempts. And even where the missionary is permitted to introduce English, the difficulties are still almost insurmountable. To learn any language well, a person must hear it spoken by people who can talk it fluently. And there would be too few for the local inhabitants to listen to. To bring in enough teachers to provide an adequate sampling of English speakers would cost, of course, much more than present methods of evangelizing the territory in its mother tongue.

Furthermore, the enormous labor involved in teaching a foreign language to thousands of illiterate people — sufficiently well that they could understand spiritual truth in it — would also take a vastly greater expenditure of missionary labor than it does for a small missionary staff to learn to converse and preach freely in the native tongue.

A similar question which arises even more frequently is this: *Why not teach the national language, or a trade language, or the lingua franca of the area instead of learning all of the dialects?*

This query cannot be easily dismissed. A great many people, in fact, are convinced that the best way of reaching the tribes of the world is through some trade language medium. To me, however, this program appears very difficult. The preacher says in Ecclesiastes 10:10: "If the iron be blunt and one do not whet the edge, then must he put to the more strength" (ARV). Even the Sword of the Spirit, though it still cuts deeply, seems to have a dull edge unless it is wielded in the language in which a man was born.

Teaching such trade languages as Spanish, French, Chinese, Malayan, or Russian would eliminate the entire problem of translating the Bible into a thousand languages which now have no part of the Scriptures whatsoever. But, though translating the Scriptures is a huge task, it does not take so much time as teaching a new language to hundreds of thousands of people. In Mexico, for example, though Spanish has been taught in the schools for about 400 years, 2,000,000 Indians still know no

Spanish; another million are "bilingual" but do not know Spanish well enough to understand it thoroughly. On the other hand, early results from translation in Mexico seem to indicate that about 150 workers could get the New Testament or some portion of it into each of the 52 languages within 25 years — and, in addition, have many people reading the Word and witnessing in each of them.

But would not a trade language permit immediate evangelization of the people who learned it, without waiting to obtain a translation?

Apparently it would. As fast as a native could learn a few words of the trade language, one could tell him of the mighty works of God.

For a long time, however, his understanding would be highly limited and subject to serious errors. Even though he heard the message in the trade language which he was learning, and appeared to absorb or repeat it, he might be mouthing verbal formulas without actually understanding. Furthermore, much of the literature available in the national languages is not in the conversational phrases learned in the remote villages. Thus, even the early advantage of the trade language is largely lost.

It should not be overlooked, or minimized, that people are more ready to respond when they hear the Word in the language which they learned in childhood and still use in the home, than when they hear the same words in a learned language.

Preaching in a trade language often arouses misunderstanding by persons who know the trade language imperfectly. Barnabas and Paul seem to have had this difficulty with people of the speech of Lycaonia (Acts 14:1-18), who could hardly be restrained from sacrificing to men.

Even in areas with considerable bilingualism, large numbers of older people and people in the back-yard areas do not know the trade language adequately or at all. It would be impossible to reach these through the trade language without a very large teaching program. If one tries to be fair to the bilinguals, in giving them the gospel rapidly, he may be even more unfair to the monolinguals — especially the older ones.

We are commanded to preach the gospel to every creature.

And we have no excuse for failing to bring the Word to these even though the task may be harder. I recall hearing the late Mr. L. L. Legters say that almost the only strong churches among the American Indians were those in which the Scriptures had been translated long ago. I have myself observed some of the Oklahoma Cherokee churches which are strong and flourishing. The members read the New Testament in the syllabary which old Chief Sequoia prepared for them.

Are not many of these tribal languages small and disappearing? Many of the languages are indeed spoken by very few people. Some of the Amazon tribes, for example, number just a few hundred. Measles or some other white man's disease could decimate the tribe. Do they not, however, have a right to hear the Word before they die? Have we not been ordered to take the Word to the uttermost parts of the world? Was the Great Commission given with the reservation that it is applicable only to tribes numbering 100,000 or more? Did not our Lord imply that one should leave the ninety and nine and go seek the one which was lost in the wilderness? Was not Philip taken from the midst of a successful revival to witness to one man? And are not some from every tribe and language going to praise His name in that Great Day?

As a matter of fact one can never be sure when a language is going to disappear. A native speaker of Albania told me recently that she came from one of two towns in Sicily which had been settled from Albania fifteen hundred years ago. One of those towns, to be sure, had lost its language and taken up Italian exclusively. Her village, however, was still an "Albanian island" in a sea of Italian speech. Recently, for another example, the American Bible Society had a request for some Iroquois Scriptures for a group of these speakers on Long Island. Some languages are extraordinarily resistant to the trade language and others are rapidly replaced by it. We cannot predict which will disappear and which will remain. The only safe way is to give all of them the Scriptures, since even those which are going to disappear are much more likely to retain a permanent church if its speakers have had the Scriptures in their own language before they have read the pagan literature of Western culture in their trade language.

If a worker is not able to stay permanently in a small tribe, but — say — for only ten years because of war conditions or health, the single, most solid contribution he can leave is something of the written Word. To leave babes in Christ with no food is not fair. To leave them the vernacular written Word with a few strong literate native leaders is to make probable their survival in the face of attacks from the Evil One.

But is not a few hundred too small a parish for the investment of a missionary life — especially if he is highly capable?

Many ministers at home, possibly a majority of them, are in churches of no more than three hundred. They contact, in addition, a few hundred people in the community, although less effectively. If they leave, someone else takes their place, working with many of these same people, so that the number of new people touched by the average minister is quite low. In addition, the pastors are almost always supported by a Sunday-school superintendent and a number of teachers of Sunday-school classes, so that the average number of persons reached compared to the number of active workers is very small indeed. Is not a tribe of two thousands buried in the jungles of the Amazon without one witness, one ray of light, or one smallest hope, an adequate field of labor for one of these same servants of the Lord? Should such a ministry give him a legitimate feeling of spiritual claustrophobia?

But are not languages too poor — how can you translate when they have no adequate vocabulary and no grammar?

One frequently hears that a language of so-called primitive people is impoverished. Such an assertion may be based upon the lack of words for certain objects which are not present among them, such as airplanes or electric lights. These blanks a living language can easily fill, either by borrowing the names from the people from whom they borrow the objects or by making up descriptive phrases — such as "flying fish" for dirigible. On the other hand one may have difficulty in finding words for certain concepts, especially abstract ones, such as "love," or "anger," or "salvation." Yet even these omissions are usually not so serious as they at first appear, since frequently the problem is one of a substituted grammatical type rather than inherent lack of the concept. In Mixtec — a language of southern Mexico — for example, we have found no nouns for "anger," "love," "hate," "joy," "fornication," and many similar words, but the people frequently say "one must not be angry," "one should love," "one should be joyful," "one should not commit fornication," and the like. That is, Mixtec uses verbs for many concepts for which English uses nouns, but they can express the same ideas.

Upon a little reflection one can see that no concepts which are restricted to Christianity could possibly be found in a language spoken only by pagans. How could pagans have developed words for Christian ideas which have never occurred to them? This identical situation existed when the Holy Spirit inspired the New Testament. At that time many pagan words, with pagan-thought background, were used in Christian contexts; by the contexts the present Christian meaning eventually built up, until it was possible to express all the Christian meaning in the pagan terms.

And it is still possible for the translator to use a similar procedure: he may choose the closest pagan equivalent and trust the Spirit to build into it a Christian concept. For example, "paradise" implies to many of us, as Christians, a state of blessed, ineffable, untranslatable bliss with Christ; yet the term in origin is "an oriental word, first used by Genophon of the parks of the Persian kings and nobles. . . . a park, pleasure-ground, garden."[1] Revelation 2:7, then, one may legitimately translate thus: "To him who conquers, I will grant to eat of the tree of life, which is in God's beautiful garden," and the Christian concept may gradually be built into it by the believers.

The grammar of any language is complex; some of them, such as Navajo, have extremely intricate types of word formation, but relatively simple phrase patterns; others, like Mixtec, tend to have the reverse. All of them have grammar amply complex to accommodate the expressions of Christian truth. Tone-rules in Mazatec (another language of Mexico), for example, are exceedingly intricate; it took the workers in the field many years to describe them adequately in preparation for their Bible translation. Every language has an intricate grammatical structure whether or not the language has a writing. It merely

1. G. Abbott Smith, *A Manual Greek Lexicon of the New Testament* (New York, 1929), p. 338.

awaits a grammarian to analyze it and write it down and then rework the Scriptures into that system.

Why then is not more vernacular preaching and translation being done?

At the moment not enough men are available. Some potential missionaries think that they are not capable of preaching in the vernacular, or producing an adequate translation, even though the average college graduate in a few months can get enough training to make it possible for him to translate with fair accuracy if he is ready to invest many years in field work afterwards. Others are able, and know it, but are waiting to be called to the uttermost corners of the earth rather than obeying the orders which Christ gave hundreds of years ago. Pray the Lord of the harvest that He will thrust forth laborers into the harvest, that every person may hear the mighty works of God in the language which he knows.

For some persons justification of the translation task for the tribes is not sufficiently answered in terms of human values. Even some Christian workers remain unmoved by the tribal need, in view of the masses of people in large exploding population centers. To me, however, in the translation task, encouragement comes from a biological-cultural analogy. From a particular kind of soil in a particular variety of climate flowers with special characteristics may spring. Each small culture provides a new human soil and climate, giving opportunity for special learning of God's mercy as it is applied to headhunter, shaman, or gardener — opportunities not available in heaven.

24 Why Angels Are Curious

SHOULD A PERSON GIVE HIS LIFE FOR A TRIBE OF 20,000 PEOPLE, or for one of 5,000, 500, or 200? Data from the Indian protection service of Brazil indicate that seventy tribes of that country have become extinct within the last fifty years. Is it worth while for a person to give his life for a tribe about to disappear? Should he sacrifice his life for just one person?

God is interested in one individual. We are so confident of His interest that we like to insert our own names into John 3:16 like this, "For God so loved the world that he gave his only begotten son, that Ken Pike believing on him hath everlasting life." Jesus wept because of one man. When Mary and Martha sent word that their brother was sick, Jesus did not ask, "Have a lot of people died? If so, I had better go around." Of course not. He said, "Lazarus is dead" (John 11:14). He was concerned with one.

Some people think in numbers. They protest, "But the tribe is so small!" They ask, "Is it worth it to go to such a small tribe?" They remember that it costs to get into the area. It is expensive transporting household equipment. It is expensive in terms of health. It is expensive in terms of time — requiring sometimes fifteen years to accomplish anything in a new culture. But in such reckoning they forget that the price of just one individual was the death of Christ.

If a small tribe is passed by because of its size, then we deny the value of the individual — he is not worth it either. If we deny the value of the individual, we are rejecting the Bible, for we are not heeding the command (Luke 14:23) to go "into the highways and hedges," the mountains, and the jungles, to reach the ones and twos that we will find there. In a sense the measure of the crucifixion is in the individual for which it was designed, and only secondarily in the masses. "Doth he not leave the ninety and nine and goeth into the mountains and seeketh that which is gone astray?" (Matthew 18:12).

God is also interested in the masses. That was the reason He sent Jonah to Nineveh, and when Jonah became disgruntled about the withered gourd, He asked (Jonah 4:11), "And should not I spare Nineveh, that great city, wherein are more than six score thousand persons?"

Jesus looked out at the crowds, the thousands, and He was moved with compassion. There were so many of them, like sheep without a shepherd. However, He was concerned not because of the "masses," but because of the men who made up the masses. Man, created in the image of God, is moved by the same things. He, too, is affected by the masses of people. Many, many workers have gone to the mission field because they realized that every tick of the clock a soul from China, India or some other land was passing into eternity. Men are also moved by the plight of the small tribes.

Even non-Christians have such sympathy. One day in Mexico City the director of the Wycliffe Bible Translators was calling on a cabinet minister. He told him that we were at his orders to go anywhere he wished. After all, why should we not? We wanted to go to all the tribes — we thought.

The cabinet minister immediately asked, "How about the Lacandons?" — a tribe of around 150 people living in a place which some of my colleagues at the University of Michigan say is the wildest place on the North American continent. He added, "None of our wives would go with us there. Would your people go there?" Here was a government official, moved with compassion for a small tribe, knowing that he did not have what it took to reach them. But he could sense that if we honestly believed in God as we affirmed that we did then that belief would take us to the 150 Indians — to live and die for them.

Our director answered, "Yes, we will be glad to go to the Lacandons."

If we had been in doubt before about whether or not it was worth it, that incident swept it all away. Either we went to that small tribe, or we denied the character of God whom we claimed to be worshipping. That was evident to the non-Christian which had been hidden from those of us who had thought we would go to the 300,000 Aztecs, or maybe to a tribe of a thousand or two, but would not bother with a tribe of 150 people.

Sometimes it costs more to help the ones and twos lost in the mountains than it does to bring home all ninety-nine from the plain. It is like mowing the lawn of a big estate. The gardener gets out the power mower and with a few times around he has cut most of the grass. Then he takes the half-mower, a hand machine with only one wheel. With that he cuts away the grass that grows next to the flower beds. But the lawn is not finished until he gets down on his hands and knees and clips the grass that is growing up against the trees. He cuts only a fraction of the grass that way but it takes more time and energy than it does to do all the rest of the lawn. Is it worth it? Well, that is the only way to have a neat, well-kept lawn.

The universe is like a lawn. The large language groups are those parts that can be cared for with the power mower. The small tribes are back against the trees where the grass is often shaggy and neglected. God wants a neat lawn and as gardners we should see to it that even the small tribes receive our attention.

Men are collectors. God, too, is a collector in the sense that He likes variety — why else did He make so many kinds of trees and snowflakes? Even in heaven there is variety. There are seraphim, "Each one had six wings; with twain he covered his face, and with twain he covered his feet, and with twain he did fly" (Isaiah 6:2). There are the "creatures" which have "four faces" and "four wings" each (Ezekiel 1:5, 6). There is also a type of "wheel." "When they went, they went upon their four sides; and they turned not when they went . . . and their rings were full of eyes round about them" (Ezekiel 1: 17, 18).

On earth each individual is different from each other individual in accordance with the struggles and victories that he has gone through here. Redeemed men are the specimens that show God's power, and His grace (Ephesians 2:7). God wants a complete collection, for man becomes a spectacle which the angels love to watch (I Corinthians 4:9 and I Peter 1:12). Why should the angels be curious? Because there is something of the grace of God that they cannot see any other way! Where in heaven can they see the mercy of God applied to a sinner? Where in heaven can they see the grace of God take a vessel of clay and fill it with power like God does with us? It cannot be seen in heaven because there is no sin there. What does an angel know experimentally about enduring persecution from fellow sinners? Nothing. What does an angel learn as he watches those of our Christian brethren who are enduring persecution? A great deal. We then are players on a stage by which the angels can learn about the love of God — things which otherwise they would never know for a million years.

No wonder there is joy in heaven over a sinner that repents. It gives the angels opportunity to see God's grace in action. The angels do not have to learn from us what it is like to be righteous. They already know that. But they do not know how it feels to be lost and have God say, "Your sins are forgiven." And when they see one of us sinners repent, they indirectly sense the thrill of it.

You say, "But that happens so often!" Yes, but it is never the same twice. God's method with me was not the one He used with you at all. If the angels see God working in me to build certain character traits, and they see Him working in you, they see different problems. They see a variety of aspects of the character of God manifested in dealing with these problems.

Now in some respects tribes are like people. Each has its

own personality, its own struggles, its own trials. Each has
its own difficulties. Therefore in the lives of Christians in different cultures there are different characteristics of God showing through. We might say that it is the same light going
through a different facet of the same diamond. It sparkles
differently. This means then that every culture has a contribution to make. Even a small culture can contribute a new
thing to the observers in heaven.

If you had five thousand orchids, all of one kind, they would
make a beautiful display. But after a visitor had looked at
them, you would take him to see just one, set apart, and say,
"This is my rarest orchid. There is only *one* of these. I had
to travel far to get it. It cost me a lot of money and time."
So also there is a museum strategy in heaven. There is more
joy in heaven over one sinner that repents than over many
others (Luke 15:7). Why? Because a convert from a small
tribe with a strange culture may be like a rare orchid. He is
an exhibit of the mercy of God poured forth in a way that
has never been seen before.

Can you not imagine God, in whose image we are created,
taking Gabriel on a guided tour? Perhaps He says, "Gabriel,
look at this one! The workers who got this one lived in the
jungle for twenty years, and they thought they had not suc-
ceeded in doing anything, but they got this individual. He is
different. I have only one of these."

Phil and Mary Baer and their children have now been living
among and witnessing to that Lacandon tribe of one hundred
and fifty people for some years. They have been in the jungle
where chewing-gum trees grow and mahogany can be used as
firewood. They have been raising their children apart from
schools, away from home, restricted to that small jungle clear-
ing. The cost has been great. But it seems worth it to them,
and it seems worth it to God. They are still sticking it out,
waiting to get their first orchid for Him.

When they do, it will mean something in heaven because for
a billion years God is going to have a showcase. For a billion
years redemption's song is going to be sung. For a billion years
He is going to use the church to show His power, His magnifi-
cence, and His glory. For a billion years it will be told not
only to man, but to the angels, to the seraphim, to the cherubim,

to all the strange looking creatures, to those funny things which have wheels with eyes within and without. And it will be to the glory of God, showing that He is not just holy, but that He is love. He is teaching it in heaven by means of redeemed sinners. And if we fail in our missionary effort, it seems to me that some facet of God's grace will not be seen.

In searching for outreach, personal struggle may find analogy in the offering of myrrh to Christ. The fragrance — frankincense — of a dedicated life in the face of personal battles, and the gold of resultant solid contribution are what we gladly have to offer. Synthesis of scholarship and devotion in our own lives will leave us content — in spite of myrrh — if it leaves behind a small deposit of His gold.

25 Gold, Frankincense, and Myrrh

"AND THEY CAME INTO THE HOUSE AND SAW THE YOUNG CHILD with Mary his mother; and they fell down and worshipped him; and opening their treasures they offered unto him gifts, gold and frankincense and myrrh" (Matthew 2:11, ARV). That is what the wise men gave the Lord. What will we place at His feet? When we stand before our Lord and when it is our turn to open our treasure chests, will we find them empty? Or will we find in them gold or frankincense or myrrh?

What is the gold which is offered to our Lord? What is it that we give to Him? Gold is solid and durable, dedicated to beauty, the result of labor, the coinage of hard work, the medium of exchange.

What is frankincense? If we were to take that from our treasure chest and offer it to our Lord, what would we be offering? It is a perfume, a fragrant life. It is character that gives the perfume to a life. It is joy which others have seen and have been encouraged by. It is love applied in service to others. It is peace and gentleness. All these are the things which make up the aroma of a lovely Christian spirit.

And myrrh . . . it is death. It is heartbreak, hopes smashed, surrender to do what we do not want to do, hardship accepted as from the hand of God. It is suffering for Christ's sake.

Gold represents a job completed. (Our Lord Himself shouted, "It is finished!" when His work had been completed.) Everytime I am in a place for any length of time, I set up a program for myself. Almost never does the Lord let me finish everything I plan, but a little while before it is too late, I stop and say, "Now, Lord, is there not something I can finish before moving on?" Something that can go into the melting pot as a bit of gold, instead of something that will be washed away unfinished?

Will we have frankincense to offer Him? II Corinthians 2:15 (Weymouth) tells us that "we are a fragrance of Christ." We are the perfume of Christ — some of us. Verse 14 tells us, "But to God be the thanks who in Christ ever leads us in His triumphal procession, displaying everywhere through us the sweetness of the knowledge of Him." That is the frankincense which we can offer to Him, a life which is fragrant with the fruits of the Spirit: love, joy, peace, gentleness. As we are, so is the aroma of Christ. And it should be fragrant; it should be attractive and sweet and pure and pleasant.

John 12:3 gives us an example of frankincense, "Then took Mary a pound of ointment of spikenard, very costly, and anointed the feet of Jesus, and wiped his feet with her hair: and the house was filled with the odour of the ointment." Mark 14:9 tells us more, "Verily I say unto you, Wheresoever this gospel shall be preached throughout the whole world, this also that she hath done shall be spoken of for a memorial of her."

What had she done? She had used some costly ointment for Christ, and our frankincense is costly too. A joyful face when we do not feel joyful costs a lot. A happy disposition, a gentle disposition, have to be bought; they do not just happen. All these things are costly, but they bring with them the fragrance of Christ, and we can present this precious perfume to Him.

Myrrh — death. "For I think, God hath set forth us the apostles last of all, as men doomed to death: for we are made a spectacle unto the world, both angels and men" (I Corinthians 4:9, ARV). "I protest by that glorying in you, brethren, which I have in Christ Jesus our Lord, I die daily" (I Corinthians 15:31, ARV).

There is no hope in this world of dying once and having the battle over. Many are they who thought that they would surrender all, that they would put all on the altar, but when they woke up the next morning they found that they had to die again that day, too. Such must die daily to desires, die daily to difficulties, to disagreements, to misunderstandings. Dying daily, they accept the will of God, and the struggle to travel the straight, narrow and stony path. And they accept that struggle as theirs by choice.

That's dying daily. That's myrrh.

It is bitter, this long-lasting spice. "For we who live are always delivered unto death for Jesus' sake" (II Corinthians 4:11, ARV). Death to our desires; life to what God wants. Death to our hopes; life to God's hopes. Death to us; life to those who hear the gospel from us. There is no escape. Every day we are given up to death, for Jesus' sake, so that the life of Jesus may be manifested in our mortal flesh. This is myrrh.

Broken with problems too big for us — "We ourselves have had the sentence of death within ourselves, that we should not trust in ourselves, but in God who raiseth the dead" (II Corinthians 1:9, ARV). We are broken that myrrh might be found in us, that we might have it on that great day when we open our treasure chest, that we might have that product of the spice of death working out in life — death to us, life to others.

Some of you are afraid that you will have nothing to offer on that great day. You look at yourselves and say, "No brains, no ability, therefore no gold and nothing to offer." Do you not realize that from such people comes the frankincense oftentimes more precious than gold? Someone has to carry the fragrance — who is going to do it? Not those of us who are supposed to be scholars but are also cold and dry and book-worms.

And then there are those people whom God chooses to take myrrh to heaven. They get to the mission field and everything goes wrong. Perhaps they get sick; they fail. They die inside long before their bodies die. And their failures hurt. And yet, committed unto God, they continue serving — with myrrh.

What do we have to offer? When we get to heaven and the Lord burns with fire the dross, will there be left a little nugget of gold, of solid work, of unlost effort? "But if any man buildeth on the foundation gold, silver, costly stones, wood, hay, stubble; each man's work shall be made manifest: for the day shall declare it" (I Corinthians 3:12, 13, ARV). In that day we will know if we have any exchange for our labor with which to make a crown of gold.

"The four and twenty elders shall fall down before him that sitteth on the throne, and shall worship him that liveth for ever and ever, and shall cast their crowns before the throne, saying, Worthy art thou, our Lord . . ." (Revelation 4:10, 11, ARV). And any crown that we have, we, too, will cast at His feet and say, "Dear Lord, worthy art Thou to take the book. This gold is nothing; just a little work. You take it." Or, "All I have is a little frankincense. You take it." Or perhaps our gift is one of myrrh, that precious gift, but one which anybody can have. Whichever the gift, we still say, "Thou art worthy . . . for thou wast slain, and hast redeemed us to God by thy blood out of every kindred, and tongue, and people, and nation" — You take it, Lord.

FLAMING CANDLE

Sharp-cut lamps of night —
By strength of Mighty God
Lighted with eternal fire,
Placed in candlestick of nought,
Roaring with energy transformed —

So we would shine,
Transformed from nothing, set apart
To light worlds with Glory
Born beneath a candle
Set o'er Bethlehem's morn.